Back to the Source:
A Gambian Journal & Memoir

The Author's Ceremonial Mandinka Mask

Back to the Source:
A Gambian Journal & Memoir

Patrick Dunn

TSL Publications

First published in Great Britain in 2021
By TSL Publications, Rickmansworth

Copyright © 2021 Patrick Dunn

ISBN
978-1-914245-47-3 (hard cover)
978-1-914245-46-6 (paper back)

The right of Patrick Dunn to be identified as the author of this work has been asserted by the author in accordance with the UK Copyright, Designs and Patents Act 1988.

All rights reserved. No part of this publication may be reproduced, stored in a retrieval system or transmitted, in any form or by any means without the prior written permission of the publisher, nor be otherwise circulated in any form of binding or cover other than that in which it is published and without a similar condition being imposed on the subsequent buyer.

Photos: copyright Patrick Dunn unless specified.

Acknowledgements

I would like to thank variously for their encouragement of my writing generally, for their contribution of ideas, for their editorial support and for their advice in bringing this book to publication - in alphabetical order:

John Carey - reader, literary critic, author and emeritus Professor of English at the University of Oxford;

Mary Conway - reader, educationalist, writer and critic;

Ros Dunn - reader, senior public servant and formerly my wife;

the late Ken Hyam - reader, educationalist, poet and photographer;

the late Foday Jibani Manka - source, Gambian National Assembly Member and local historian at Janjanbureh;

Nicole Seymour-Smith - reader and confidante;

Peter Straus - literary agent - Managing Director RCW;

Begay Thorp - a Gambian source;

Dr Justin Woodman - source and anthropologist - senior lecture and senior tutor Goldsmiths, University of London.

For my daughters Lillie, Alice and Olivia without whom my life would be immeasurably the poorer and for the Marongs and the Bahs, my *kunda* folk with whom I shared my life in Janjanbureh from September 2010 to December 2012

'The longer I live the more convinced I become that one of the greatest honours we can confer on other people is to see them as they are, to recognise not only that they exist, but that they exist in specific ways and have specific realities.'

(Shiva Naipaul)

Prelude

When you transplant yourself due south and a little west from London approximately 3000 miles to the rural West African interior to share the life of its people for a prolonged period, you don't just move to a different place geographically and climatically, you enter a world with completely different methodologies, a different tradition of explanation with its own narratives, its own interpretation of human and animal behaviour, its own understanding of natural phenomena, its own sensitivities and values and its own modi operandi. It is a world not readily accessible to the post-enlightenment comprehension of our contemporary western minds. If you don't meet this world with receptivity, with modesty, with a spirit of cultural exploration – and leave didacticism behind – you will learn nothing, you will miss everything of value and you will fail to understand what they have that we have not. But be warned, if you can do this, Africa may claim a part of you as its own!

In July 1730 Francis Moore was appointed as a 'writer' [clerk] by the Royal African Company on a three year contract and left London on 2 September of that year bound for the company's trading establishments on the Gambia River. In the spring of 2010 I accepted an offer from an international development charity to serve a one year placement 180 miles upriver as an education management advisor in the Central River Region of The Gambia – departing on 12 August.

We met in a broad beam of blended light coming through the glass wall of the departure lounge in one Heathrow terminal or another ... that is the other volunteers and I. The light had been filtered through an early morning August sky filled with the shimmering exhalations of jet engines as they pushed their loads along runways or up into the infinite blue above. There were a dozen or so of us who identified one another from the memory of a face encountered during a residential, pre-departure training weekend or from having seen a participant's photo posted during an online prep course or simply by the tell-tale motorcycle crash helmet sticking awkwardly out of another's hand luggage. We shared not only a common destination but also no doubt the sense of a current life broken off precipitously. For me during the steep ascent at take-off that morning, the falling away of so many of my routine daily preoccupations and responsibilities was tangible and liberating. This immediate personal feeling was mixed too with a feeling of regret that I would not only be remote from family and friends but also unable to observe more immediately the then just commenced experiment – unique in UK post-war terms – in coalition government. I knew that once I had arrived at my destination my communication with the outside world would be severely limited. I did not know that I would also feel closer to the Source – closer to the beginning of our human journey.

Into Africa!

After a transfer at Brussels, capital city of a country linked with some of the darkest European connections with the African past – and a brief stop at Dakar – we stepped off the plane at Banjul and walked into a wall of dry heat. It felt as if the air stream from a giant fan heater on its maximum heat-setting was trained across the aircraft's cabin doorway. However by the time we had travelled the short distance to customs and the baggage hall via a five-minute bus ride across an airfield only sparsely populated with a few aircraft, vehicles and dilapidated buildings – giving a distinctly banana republic feel – the sensation had changed. It had become clear that the dry heat was not dry at all and that what we were experiencing was more like walking into a shower room after someone had taken a very long and hot shower. Rivulets of sweat trickled down my face. Here, in what some might regard as the fag-end of Africa, it was the middle of the wet season with intense humidity levels that would not fall until mid-October.

Francis Moore arrived off Cape St Mary in the Royal African Company sloop *Dispatch* on 9 November 1730. The *Dispatch* weighed anchor in the mouth of the Gambia River. Moore was en-route to the fort on James Island twenty-five miles upriver which he reached two days later. Fort James was the key staging post for goods traded by the Royal African Company travelling into and out of the interior.

Moore tells us that:

I kept the journal when in Gambia, not with any design of printing it, but to improve myself, and keep in my mind the things worth notice.

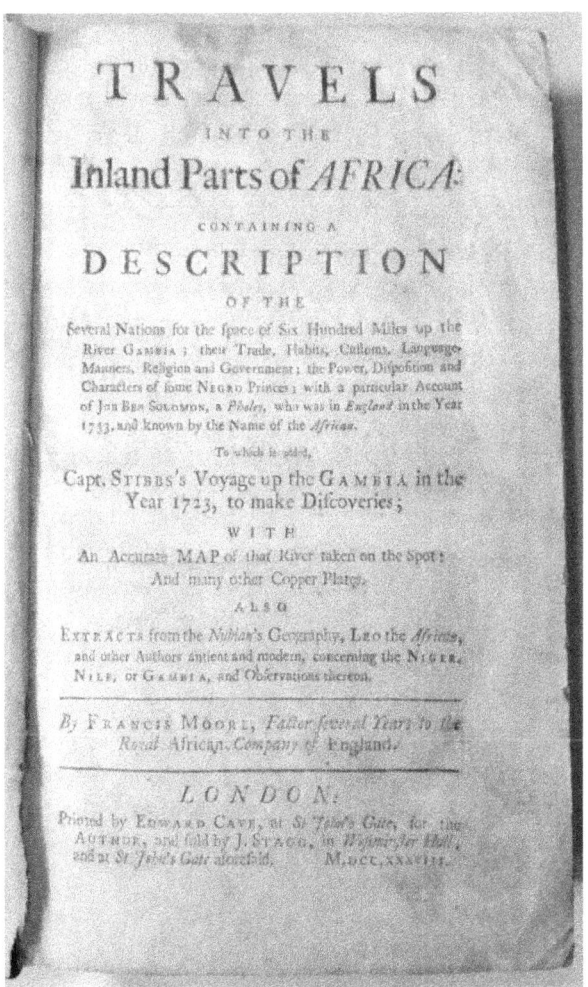

The title-page of Francis Moore's Book published 1738

My journal for 12.08.2010 records:

> ... **arrived Banjul** to commence approximately three weeks training on the coast before being sent up-country to my placement. Currently we are in the wet season and it is very hot and humid. I am told that in fact it is very hot all the year round. The humidity levels here on the coast have to be experienced to be believed and several changes of clothes a day would be ideal but also impractical ...
>
> In the baggage hall we experienced a scrum for luggage and uninvited offers of help came from all directions from unknown Africans - each expressed as if from a long lost friend. Our group together with other recent arrivals created a kind of feeding frenzy of opportunity for gain for this first melee of chancers we encountered - my first experience of the fabled 'bumsters' we had been warned about during our NGO's pre-departure briefings etc. Their incorrigibility was impressive.

After baking in the heat for 30 minutes or so outside the main terminal building with our baggage whilst waiting for our transport to arrive, a small convoy of trucks appeared and we were loaded aboard. We had been told this convoy and its staff complement would be there to greet us when we landed but I was soon to learn that nothing happens very promptly in this part of West Africa and that here such a short delay as this could be regarded as Promptitude itself.

At points on route from the airport to our hotel we passed through streets thronging with people and business activities which, as in other tropical locations I have visited, seemed to be conducted entirely alfresco. There were streets lined with shops selling cheaply produced and showy chairs, tables, beds and sofas ... then a patch of shops selling ancient computers spread out on a few rickety tables ... then a series of market stalls selling foodstuffs and so on.

An early journal entry records:

> ... one thing that strikes you coming here from the West is just how ramshackle, decaying, re-cycled, unfinished and impoverished everything is. Many of the roads are dirt

roads, including long stretches of the few main roads and there seem to be almost never any pavements - even in the urban areas - except in Banjul the capital but even here only some of the time. In town and country, goats, sheep, chickens and dogs roam freely in the streets ... one wonders how their owners ever find them ... one imagines there must be endless proprietorial disputes!

Although we were journeying through, in local terms, an urban area of relatively high density, always and everywhere the bush seemed to be fighting a battle to re-establish its natural right to the land. Buildings, roads and other urban structures had plants and trees forcing their way around, between and through them and intermittently there would be large patches of land where the developers seemed to have given up their human endeavours to tame the land altogether and the bush had regained its ancient supremacy.

My journal continues:

On our journey between the airport and the hotel we were delayed by a contra-flow arrangement which eventually brought us to a standstill outside **the local abattoir**. For a moment the fanciful and frightening idea passed through my mind that perhaps by some accident of planning, or by sinister design, our journey had taken us to a culturally atavistic region where cannibalistic demands meant that we were to be the next consignment to be processed! In fact I soon noticed that the roadsides were full of sheep milling around with some cattle too - all awaiting their inexorable fate. Police and troops controlled all movements of traffic and people. The troops were coming and going in full combat gear standing as densely packed as possible in army trucks - each soldier with his gun at the ready. Large groups of them poured out of or sardined themselves into the trucks as if a liquid human flow. Inside our NGO vehicle warnings circulated from our African escorts not to take photographs or we might risk at the very least the confiscation of our cameras. Eventually our driver explained that the President himself was in attendance at the abattoir, in fact *his* abattoir, to set the national price of meat and that His Excellency, whose full title was inordinately long, was about to leave. When eventually he did, his convoy of Hummers issued forth from the abattoir gates in dramatic fashion with rocket launchers, machine guns and other hardware mounted onto customised platforms which were integrated into the vehicles' coachworks. As these Hummers accelerated away bizarrely packets of biscuits sprayed out of them to be scrambled for by the watching children and others. The regime in all its biscuit beneficence therefore could be seen to care truly for its people. I later learned that this was a signature gesture of the President's, commonly witnessed and which on occasion claimed the lives of the children who might take undue risks to claim their prizes by getting too close to the wheels of His Excellency's ostentatiously speeding convoy.

Eventually we reached our hotel which had been arranged for us for the first few days of our NGO's in-country induction. It was located up a dirt side road in **Fajara** amidst some urban development just set back from the coastal strip. At the heart of this small complex was a rectangular pool for bathing, bordered at one end by the main hotel building and along one side by a terrace of self-contained rooms. I was allocated one of these rooms. The garden that ran between our terrace and the edge of the pool, though relatively narrow, was dense with mature and lush trees and shrubs including palms and many other exotic species. It was visited by the local very varied bird life – adding brilliant splashes of the most vibrant colour to the thick verdure. Each time I passed through this border along one of the short pathways that intersected it to give access to the pool from my room, I felt as if I had walked into one of those extraordinarily vivid and crowded canvases by Henri Rousseau.

For our group the hotel was in fact just a staging post that offered relative luxury for a few days prior to our being hardened-off in less hospitable, self-catering accommodation for three or four weeks as preparation for subsequent life at our various final destinations. In many cases this would be far away up-country. But even before the next move, the local conditions began to make themselves felt. Not only did some of our party seem to provide a ready and eager meal for much of the local insect life which inhabited the lush vegetation of the hotel garden but we suffered too from the intense heat and humidity. We were well into the tropics with no air-conditioning and had fans only when power supplies were forthcoming. On the first night I went through a series of decisions which had not been necessary back home. Should the windows be left open or closed, balancing security against heat discomfort? Should the curtains be left open or closed, balancing privacy against air flow? Would anyone complain about the profligacy of my leaving the fan on all night? [I was enough of a novice not to realise that we were expected to do this.] In bed after carefully tucking in my mosquito net under the mattress from the inside – a skill which was to become second nature to me – I had difficulty in getting to sleep and when I eventually managed to do so it was at a level of consciousness only marginally below that of my awake state. In the early hours I came to the surface again with my whole body running with sweat and feeling as if I was sleeping in a swamp. In my state of naivety I did not realise that this would be the pattern of my sleep almost every night for the next year and a half that I was to spend in West Africa.

Settling in on the Coast

In those early days on the coast there were constant unscheduled power cuts which would throw us into darkness at the most inopportune moments, such as when we were at one of the local restaurants just as our evening meal had been served or even worse just as it had been ordered. In the latter circumstances I could only wonder at, and feel humbled by, the ingenuity of the kitchen staff who somehow invariably managed to complete the production of the food ordered. Of course at this end of the country near to the capital and tourist centres some establishments had their own generators which would kick in to relieve the power situation – if and when such generators were in running order and had adequate fuel supplies to be operable. But many of the establishments we frequented ran on a shoestring by the sheer ingenuity of their proprietors and workforce and had no such equipment to which they could resort. Large groups would be catered for through the use of wind-up or battery operated lanterns or just candlelight. Cooking in terms of the heat required would be largely unaffected as it was mainly undertaken on wood fires – but often with very little light.

The second day here and we have been to our organisation's 'In-country' HQ situated on a road just set back from the coast. This road is populated mainly by buildings containing the offices of other national and international agencies and delegations. **Our HQ** is based in a yellow ochre bungalow a short distance from the British High Commission and almost opposite the Medical Research Council - an independent medical research organisation set up in and primarily funded by the UK.

... The hand-shaking with our male HQ staff, whether we had already met them or not, went on interminably. This was followed by equally interminable form filling as a prelude to a modular training programme intended to familiarise us with local cultural sensitivities, living conditions and other skills and knowledge needed.

Programme content includes when to and when not to shake hands with women, how to use a pit latrine and how to brew *atiya* (a very sweet green tea concoction the making of which is often seen as somewhat disreputable). There will also be sessions giving us a basic introduction to the relevant tribal language required for our particular placement. In my case this is Mandinka - for some others Fula or Wolof. We adjourned for lunch which for me was a light prawn and groundnut stew with the inevitable rice. We finished our day earlier than scheduled and went back to the hotel.

Apparently there is a view here that this early stage of volunteer acclimatisation/training can have too softening an effect for what lies ahead up-country where there can be severe limitations on fresh food supply. The movement of produce to more remote destinations is said to be made worse by an under-utilisation of the great river and the impassable roads in the wet season.

We have begun a programme of visits to some of the more notable local sights and attractions here in the coastal area around the capital.

Create a palette of ochre, indigo, crimson, burnished gold, marine hues of turquoise, sienna, humming bird blue, aquatint, verdigris, royal purple, brilliant white, emerald green and then add as many more again and again of the most exotic and vivid shades of colour that you can imagine - this was the variety of colour on display in the garb of the African women and men present. Imagine too experiencing an olfactory variety no less diverse though at times less pleasant including that of freshly caught fish beginning to turn in the fierce heat, the odour of bodies that have toiled long in the sun, the smell of spices and incense unfamiliar in The West. To this add an equally diverse range of human activity packed into narrow alleyways and at the edges of busy dirt roads apparently blessed with a human navigation system to compare well with that of a bats at dusk so as to avoid any major collisions or dysfunction of movement - all this bathed in the hum of unremitting chatter and other human discourse which to the unfamiliar ear moulds itself into one undulating and unbroken stream of sound. If you can imagine all this you will have some idea of the experience of a mid-afternoon walk through **Serrekunda Market**...

Night 3: Power cuts - no lights; no fans - especially uncomfortable as no means of keeping cool at night so as to sleep. And oh yes no water supply so no means of washing - apparently shortages such as these are common here.

Day 4:... **Visit to St Paul's Church, Fajara (Anglican)**... the liturgy seems perfectly familiar (coming here as a practising Anglican from an Anglo Catholic tradition) with Bishop Solomon Tilewa Johnson officiating. Amongst the congregation there were a few Westerners including an honoured guest from the USPG (an Anglican missionary organisation) - in her straw hat with its hat-band she was every inch the epitome of the 1930s prim colonialist. She was officially welcomed and given a special blessing by his Right Reverend.

I received Communion in two kinds - not sure about the wine - thought it might have been off. The service lasted two-and-a-quarter hours. We arrived late for it however and having been soaked through by a sudden shower en route. The fierce overhead fans, there to combat the heat, dried us out completely during the 45 minutes of the service left to run. Our fellow worshippers were forbidding - smart and generally well turned-out African ladies with vivid frocks and head scarves [*mulfi*] and African men in well pressed suits and ties - this my first formal encounter in West Africa with my brothers and sisters in Christ.

Day 4 (contd) ... A light lunch followed by an afternoon swim in the pool ... no water for washing or flushing until evening approached. Our group eventually adjourned more or less en bloc for the evening to a recently established restaurant come ex-pat/NGO community centre called **The Scottish Embassy**. It was situated in a small compound a short distance down a dirt road off the Bakau Road. There were more power cuts with just a couple of wind-up lamps to illuminate our evening meal which had to be produced in darkness. The lamps seemed to attract all manner of mainly flying insects in massive quantities. The lack of power and light resulted in a restricted menu offer. I went for the cassava stew with a fiery hot sauce which turned out to be excellent. We ate under a grass roof whilst a Scottish flag hung limply nearby in the windless evening. Entertainment laid on consisted of an African singer/drummer who alternated with recorded and completely incongruous Scottish music which seemed even more out of place because I don't think any of us understood the Scottish connection. There was general relief when the power returned towards the end of our meals and we were able to see what we'd been eating. A far as I know there were no unpleasant surprises. When we returned to the hotel it was a relief to learn that the water supply was just beginning to be re-established ...

... I have been monitoring myself carefully to check that I am recovering from a minor operation I underwent in the UK at the end of July just prior to departure. I now feel that I should be ok before undertaking the trip up country ...

There is much talk within our group about the best phone and internet links to use to keep in contact with our families and friends back home. For those going up-country careful thought must be given to network coverage which varies greatly from one company to another apparently ...

... News has just been received that two seasoned volunteers from an earlier cohort - the colleagues who showed us around the market and elsewhere - have gone down with heat stroke for their efforts. One is on a drip - pleasant Aussie female colleague with whom I chatted in the *gelleh-gelleh* [large mini-bus type vehicle, varying sizes for between about 10 and 20 people] on the way back from the market trip. Hope she's ok! The other from Wales and equally nice, has been unwell for a week or two apparently and perhaps should not have offered her services for our training - she's seriously dehydrated it is thought.

... more established volunteers than ourselves have reported that formerly, as part of their in-country training, new arrivals used to be sent out to local villages near the coast for a period to get a taste of what was to come up-country. Reputedly the practice has now changed as the attrition rate was high and some had to be repatriated even before they reached their permanent destinations. This is beginning to sound too seriously challenging and I feel it can't be right as surely it would have prompted a discontinuance of up-country postings altogether ... uh wouldn't it? I am reminded that earlier writers have referred to West Africa as 'the white man's grave'.

Moore's journal is peppered with accounts of the loss of company colleagues due wholly or partly to the adverse conditions. When you weigh up the advances since his time and consider the immediacy of accessibility to them in many parts of this country today, especially during the wet season, you realise that they boil down really to very few things, key though they are, such as filtered water for drinking and anti-material preventative and remedial medication ...

> ... a sluggish day of training at the premises of the NGO umbrella organisation during which event I was supposed to meet a representative from the regional directorate with which I will be working up-country ... but they didn't show! Went back to the hotel and then took a walk along the beach at Fajara to fill in the time before dinner. A hundred metres wide strip of soft, white sand stretching into the far horizon in both directions along the water's edge bounded by a line of coconut palms to its landward edge and the breaking white surf to seaward ... all beneath cotton wool clouds set in a brilliant blue sky. Sometimes here it can be easy to count one's blessings!
>
> Back to the hotel for our evening meal and more power cuts ...
>
> ... today I learnt that this is the second day of Ramadan which seems to be strictly observed by almost everyone including sometimes non-Muslim Gambians who observe the fast out of respect for their fellow countrymen and women. Our small group of volunteers similarly decides to eat discreetly during the day and not to knock back the first of their ice cold bottles of lager until after the break of fast. Given that most Muslims here don't drink alcohol anyway I think it quite possible that this partial abstinence is lost on them. 'Julbrew' is the locally brewed lager based on German lager-making know-how – a bottle, often followed by another, slips down rather too easily in the intense heat – no doubt giving short term relief but making the over-heating problem worse in the longer term ...

... Decided to have dinner at a small restaurant in Fajara with the most excellent fresh homemade meat pies at 35 dalasi (approx 75p in UK money) Tables are almost all outside. It turned out to be the night upon which swarms of a particular insect species unknown to me – resembling a dragonfly but smaller and sleeker – took to the wing. We are told that like mayflies they have a very short lifespan, in fact flying for one day only. After dark, each lamppost attracted clouds of these flying creatures numbering in the tens of thousands. In the restaurant forecourt under an awning, our plates of food were dive-bombed at regular intervals by them. We knocked them away and as they fell stunned to the floor one or more of the dozens of frogs, which were stationed singly every couple of yards or so around our feet, would hop forward and efficiently and quickly devour all except the wings – practised in this operation as they obviously were. The following day I saw a carpet of these wings under each lamppost, as if an autumn squall had deposited drifts of leaves around the trunk of each tree in an English wood. This was now the only trace that remained of the myriad insects that had been on the wing just the evening before ...

... Today **the transition to rougher conditions begins** and the group is divided into smaller batches and sent to various locations. Mine, a group of six, is allocated a dilapidated house up a dirt track off a street called 'Pipeline' in **Kanifing**. It is one of the quirks of nomenclature here that the titles of streets and other notable locations can be so descriptively literal. It is as if a great collective lapse in the imaginative faculty occurred amongst those responsible at the time of their official naming. 'Pipeline' the street follows the course of an arterial water main. Other examples include a junction called 'Traffic-Lights', another called 'Post Office' (guess what's on the corner?) and another called 'Turntable' (which means roundabout here) and guess what you drive around at this point? ...

... At our new accommodation almost nothing is without defect. Everything is shoddily constructed and there are doors that don't close properly, locks on bathroom doors that don't work - a kitchen tap which usually emits no water and when it does the water seems to run down the back of the sink and onto the floor, pipework with leaks at various points along its length, roof leaks with water dripping from the ceiling in various places, broken door hinges, mosquito nets that are so old they have gone brown with age and with all traces of their impregnated chemical repellent having long since become ineffective. There are showers but if you try to use them after about 7.30 in the morning they have run dry because of the general inadequacy of the water supply to the district in which our house is located. Frequently therefore for the purposes of washing one resorts to a bucket and scoop, in the native manner, which is why we take it in turns to fill the buckets and jerry cans when supplies become available - which is almost always late in the day and from the standpipe behind the house. There is of course no hot water. In the back yard we are blessed with a mature grapefruit tree. To get to it you have to tramp through an overgrown and partly paved backyard inhabited by very large ants with a painful bite.

We have a cleaner who appears every few days. She makes the place look as best it can. The beds are made, our clothes are washed (for which we pay her extra) and she sprays the insect life to keep it at bay until her next visit.

The dirt road on which our house is situated has no street lamps. After dark it is difficult to negotiate especially after one of the frequent downpours as large and deep puddles form everywhere. The habit of carrying a torch begins to establish itself with many of us.

... In the vicinity of our house as elsewhere, dogs, goats, chickens and occasionally donkeys wander hither and thither or are tethered whilst grazing. When you look at the mainly bare roadside earth you wonder what they find to eat. Of course the answer is anything and everything. On a number of occasions I have seen sheep and goats eat street litter and other objects normally regarded as inedible ...

...We have a **security guard** day and night - one for each shift. They are meant to patrol the compound to ensure that there are no break-ins etc. However the one who works the night shift usually spends the night sleeping on the sofa in the sitting room. We are not sure that he's supposed to do that ...? When we offered him a substantial bowl of nuts left lying around for anyone to snack on casually he thanked us politely and then proceeded to eat the whole bowl. My guess is that he's not familiar with the concept of casual snacking.

Looking back now I wonder whether he was just generally hungry. On one occasion we reported to him that after dark sometimes a rat would appear in the garden and on the veranda [there were probably several]. The following day he turned up for work with an improvised rat trap. It had been made from an empty, rectangular, gallon oil can. Its base had been removed and somehow turned into a swinging one-way entrance flap. He said he intended to catch the rat and eat it. We were slightly taken aback by this. A few days later when I asked him whether he had had any success he said 'Yes' and rubbing his stomach indicated that the rat had been very good eating.

... It is a mystery to me how Gambians keep their vehicles on the road given their dilapidated state. They are absolute wrecks with springs coming through seats, suspension completely shot, dents, rot, doors that barely open, windows stuck open or closed etc ...

... **there are little kiosks come small shops called** *bitiks*. They peep out of the sides of dwellings or form part of a wall along the roadside. They usually have a small corrugated tin awning with a couple of timber pillars to support it to provide a cover above a serving hatch. Unlike small shops in the West sprouting bright and clear signage, they are very dull and dowdy and therefore inconspicuous. They blend into the façade in which they have been integrated almost as if camou-flaged. Anyone unfamiliar with this urban facility and landscape can easily walk past them without noticing they are there but eventually the eye becomes trained to pick them out. They sell typically basic commodities such as eggs, sugar, powdered milk, freshly baked bread twice a day and other foodstuffs with cigarettes, phone credit etc. Often the serving hatch is formed of chicken wire nailed to a crude wooden frame with a small aperture at counter level through which customers can pass their money in exchange for their purchases. Presumably this is a security measure against potential thieving, though to the Western eye the meagre stock value and quantity seems hardly to warrant this. The over-all effect of these usually very grimy looking basic grocery shops is more like an old garden shed and before one examines their stock more carefully one fully expects so see oil cans, rags, pruning shears and the like within ...

Week 2: ... and before I can feel smug in any way about my ability to cope with the extreme conditions here I have been diagnosed with **suspected malaria, a blood disorder and** the inevitable and euphemistically named, **travellers' tummy**. I have been referred to the medical support organisation sub-contracted by my own organisation ... but health care here, even when supposedly top of the range, seems to be very basic by our standards ... following a series of injections, I have been prescribed two sorts of antibiotics with some malarial treatment, plus something called 'PCM' paracetamol I think + multi-vitamins ... I have been feverish and weak and spent most of my time for a couple of days now in my bed just resting and sleeping.

Francis Moore records early in his journal that:

... I was very ill with pains in my bones and boils breaking out all over me so that for four days I was scarce able to crawl ...

My outbreak of traveller's tummy is by no means unique within our group. For several days now I have been receiving many unsolicited, direct and indirect reports of the bowel movements of other group members. In fact never in the field of human bowel movements can there have been so many such reports circulating in so short a period of time across such a small group of people. There are those amongst us who insist on promulgating this information which I find unnecessary and would rather not receive. One colleague is of the view that Wanja juice, a deep burgundy coloured drink made from the dried flowers of the sorrel plant, is a particular hazard in instigating this problem and should be avoided.

Commonly now accounts are circulating amongst colleagues about the difficult conditions up-country and the non-availability of quite ordinary commodities. One feels all the more concerned given that even here in the supposedly less demanding coastal area one has already been challenged by the tremendous heat and the regular and torrential downpours.

Moore tells us:

... This is the rainy season in which it is very difficult to send goods to upper factories ...

Further, all too frequently, one witnesses the dehumanising battle fought against poverty by many of the local population, often in extreme squalor and one wonders how this plays out for people further up-river.

We have each been given a budget to spend on basic household items and foodstuffs to take with us on our journey up-country to get us started. All has to be transported and carried as necessary to its final destination as part of our luggage.

... been here now for 3/4 weeks only though so much has happened to me that it feels as if I have been away for months. I am glad to note that I now seem to have fully recovered from my various ailments ...

... I am beginning to get plugged into some of **the ex-pat community** that exists here. Much of it is Western but not all. There are various NGO staff especially Americans, Australians, Scandinavians, Brits, Filipinos and Africans from other parts of this continent, especially Ugandans. There are too other employees and secondees on fixed term contracts engaged as teachers at the University, at local Colleges and as doctors/medical assistants at the MRC (Medical Research Council). There is for example a young female Indo-Norwegian studying maternal mortality rates for six months – she is going up-country to her hospital posting at Farafenni shortly. There are also a few entrepreneurs and other business men and women. These various ex-pats will often coalesce in an unplanned way in cafes, restaurants, internet shops in the evening or at weekends as they bump into one another. Additionally one finds quite a number of Europeans of various nationalities who have chosen to spend their retirement here as their money goes a long way and very much further than back home in their country of origin. As a result of the presence of both these groups and the propensity for those far from home to gravitate towards others in similar circumstances, one frequently finds oneself with unexpected drinking companions.

... those amongst my volunteer colleagues who are expected to use a **motorbike** on placement are undergoing **an intensive week long course** ... I am one of them. We have to learn to drive on sand, unmade roads, through deep puddles and essentially through the bush. Many colleagues have no previous experience except that gained via a short course in the UK before departure. In my case I have had a one-day UK refresher programme having been a regular motorcyclist previously ... though that was some 40 years ago .

... I have sustained a couple of unpleasant grazes and bumps having come off my motor bike twice during training. Riding off-road is not easy ... especially on rutted and waterlogged roads or deep sand.

Today along with some volunteer colleagues, a few passing tourists and various African locals **I helped some fishermen at Bakau land their catch**. Their fishing method involved paying out from the stern of their long-boat a long, shallow net whilst the boat completed an arc along the coast from one point on the beach to another a little further along. The idea was that anything within the arch would be trapped. The role of the helpers on the beach ... I was one of them ... was to haul the ends of the net back into the shore. There were about 30 of us on each end of the net. The catch was meagre indeed, with only a few dozen or so fish landed along with a few crabs which the fishermen dealt with by ripping off their large claws and then stuffing the poor creatures, still wriggling, into their trouser pockets. However there was one creature of note, at once large and exotic - this was **a magnificent green turtle**. As the arch of the net grew smaller with its farthest perimeter becoming ever nearer to the shore, this creature's head and back became clearly visible. Two of the fishermen waded out into the shallows to capture it. Each man took hold of a front and back flipper and steered the turtle up onto the beach. It must have been about four feet long and about two and a half feet wide. Once the beach was attained it was flipped over onto its back so that it was unable to move. In this upside down state the creature continued to struggle by moving its flippers backwards and forwards frantically until its strength began to fail and its head began to sink backwards and downwards towards the ground. I was struck first by the brutal indignity of the turtle's situation, by the terror and ultimately the resignation in its huge, deep eyes and the contrast between this and the complete lack of concern from the fishermen who had engineered its desperate plight.

There was great consternation amongst many of the tourists and other onlookers who witnessed this scene and the fishermen offered to let the turtle go in exchange for an unspecified sum of money. At once a debate ensued amongst our volunteer group raising such questions as: 'Should not this time-honoured activity be allowed to take its course?' ... ah ... assuming it is such an activity that is. Weren't some of us expressing greater sympathy with the plight of the turtle than with the plight of the fishermen and was this right? Wouldn't the fishermen prefer the money to the turtle meat anyway? Was the creature on the protected species list? Ultimately this jamboree of questions and the variety of views expressed in response produced no consensus or way forward and so by default the creature was left to its fate.

It is now the end of August and **the wet season continues**. We have just had the third power cut today. The natural elements are never far from winning an all-out victory over the human effort to survive against them. It is evening and the lights of the café we have gravitated to tonight have dimmed, the counter-cabinet lamps are flickering and the air conditioning system is barely throwing out any cool air now that the establishment is reliant on its own inefficient generator. Like them our volunteer group flags and fades and we melt away making an early departure into the outer darkness and up the dirt tracks back to our various lodgings ...

04.09.10: Today, with a group of volunteer colleagues, I went along to **Independence Stadium** in **Bakau** to give support to the Gambian national football team who were playing Namibia in an African Cup of Nations qualifier. There was a sense amongst us that we wanted to show our allegiance to our host nation; to our newly adopted home. We went with some trepidation having been told by our NGO HQ during in-country training that pickpockets commonly operated in crowded places. One of our number, a volunteer colleague named Marcus, did his best to remind us all of this, in paternal manner, both before we left home and again as we entered the Stadium area so as to sharpen our vigilance. He reminded us that as 'toubabs' [the name in The Gambia for those of European descent] we would stand out and be regarded as good pickings by these skilful operators who often worked in packs. I pushed my Blackberry phone down as far as I could into the front pocket of my tight jeans so that I could feel its presence next to my thigh. Negotiating one or two crowded gangways and staircases we were lucky to find our way to some very good seats towards the front. Our vociferous support was rewarded with an excellent first half display from the home team who went 3-0 up by half-time.

I was confident that I had avoided having anything stolen because I had been so much on my guard and I had felt nothing. When I put my hand in my pocket to reach for my phone similarly I felt nothing! The phone had gone without the slightest sensation being felt by me! I decided there was no action I could take immediately to retrieve the situation and settled down with irritation and self-admonition to watch the second half of the match.

At full time as we left the stadium I decided to admit to colleagues that somehow foolishly I had become a pickpocket victim. As others unburdened themselves one by one it emerged I was far from alone. Of the twenty-one of us in our group no fewer than nine owned up to having had something stolen - one a credit card, another a mobile phone, another a passport and so on. As we made our way home it felt like participating in a scene that might have been captured by Hogarth entitled 'The Return of the Fleeced!' or some such. Marcus, the colleague who had been pre-eminent in reminding us of the dangers that awaited us at the Stadium had by now sunk into a despondent silence. Sensitive questioning established that he had been relieved of his phone, his camera and his wallet containing all his key cards and documents.

The final score: The Gambia 3 Namibia 1.

This very same Marcus, as our group's IT specialist, was invaluable in ensuring that our various personal computers [laptops, iPads, notebooks etc.] were fully protected against viruses and all manner of threats to them. Marcus downloaded and set up for us anti-spyware, virus protection, firewalls and the like. It seemed rough justice therefore that on only his second or third day at his up-country placement and after assiduously ensuring the front door of his house in his compound had been locked before leaving for a trip to the local market, his own computer disappeared without trace, protective software and all. It transpired that whilst the front door was locked he had left the back door open believing that the enclosed, private, high-walled latrine/back yard area that it gave access to was sufficiently impenetrable. It was of course easily scaled by anyone with sufficient intent.

One is tempted to say one must always take care of the basics first!

The Journey Up-Country

... after some uncertainty and shifting of the original schedule the move up-country has now been fixed for 7th September ... For this first trip transport will be laid on by our NGO especially because we will be moving with not only our ordinary luggage but all the equipment necessities that each of us has been purchasing with the small allowance given to us by our organisation ...

In my party there are four of us plus a driver. We have been allocated one of our organisation's pick-up trucks. The vehicle is piled high with our personal luggage and other equipment. This has a rope to secure it and a plastic cover to keep everything dry. We are being billeted one by one to a string of placements reaching further and further up-country. In our party I am the last to be dropped off at the furthest point east. The intention has been for us to get an early start so that all destination points can be reached in one day's drive. A needless administrative delay involving the driver awaiting signatures to access cash for the petrol that he will need to purchase en route ensures that departure cannot take place until midday and therefore an over-night stay will be necessary in my case before I can reach my final destination.

Setting out at last we need first to cross the river estuary from **Banjul's port area to the ferry point at Barra on the opposite bank.** We can then work our way east along the north bank of the river. Our party contains volunteers who are to be billeted to settlements on both the north and south banks so we need to cross back to the south bank further upstream. At the first and main ferry point, once an incoming ferry arrives, the chaos of unloading and reloading is profound. There is much queue jumping with and without official consent. There are gelleh-gellehs with goats lashed to their roofs and sometimes various other vehicles advancing up the dock's unloading/loading ramp and then reversing to their original position – sometimes quantities of foot passengers are allowed to board and sometimes not. Eventually I begin to understand that the ferrymen are trying to identify a vehicle heavy enough to weigh down the dock-loading ramp sufficiently to ensure that it can engage and lock with the ferry's exit/loading ramp, as in the positions they assume naturally they seem not to be aligned. Many things that facilitate our crossing both in process and infrastructure seem sub-standard. I learned later that accidents and ferry breakdowns are not infrequent and sometimes fatal.

Once the ramp is secured and the vehicles loaded there is a general free-for-all with a minor stampede of foot passengers looking for the best and most comfortable vantage points on-board. They are carrying all manner of things on their heads, around their shoulders, in wheelbarrows and in hand-carts such as livestock (especially goats and chickens), carpets, materials, mattresses, market produce etc. At last we set sail and manage to reach the other side safely.

Towards the close of day, after leaving one colleague at our first drop off point and then two more on the south bank after a further ferry crossing, our journey is broken until morning. I am shown to my room in a guesthouse just east of **Soma** [a short distance downstream from Elephant Island].

It has shiny green walls, a blue-green and red patterned ceiling with stains all over it. There is an oscillating ceiling fan and my bed has a crude headboard of cheap carved and painted wood. There are no sheets on the bed and one very thin pillow (even though the bed is a double bed). There is a flush loo but no loo paper in a grimy bathroom with no shaving mirror. More worryingly the bed has no mosquito net. Except for this last issue which is very concerning this accommodation is several times better than that which I have just left on the coast.

... One night we anchored off Elephant Island; from whence we had a vast number of mosquitoes and sand flies who diverted us so prettily that we could not get any sleep all night. On the 4th September we reached Joar but I was so miserably mauled on the way by mosquitoes that I could hardly walk from the boat up to the factory ...

so writes Francis Moore about this locale on his own journey upcountry.

Given the mosquito net situation when retiring to bed I leave on the light and try to stay to some degree on guard. I therefore move into and out of a very light sleep contemplating the fan during my more wakeful periods as it rotates the night-time hours away with my mind drawing closer to its more primal haunts whence I sink a little below the level of waking consciousness.

We start fairly early the following day. So far the country has been very lush - the constant downpours have been particularly heavy for the last two or three days and the fierce temperatures have fallen a little over the same period. The terrain here has a strange familiarity for me - not of course through its flora and fauna but because it is almost entirely without high ground or indeed any significant undulation. It generates thoughts of those wonderfully big skies that I associate with my East Anglian childhood and youth ...

There are too, oddly and occasionally, right out in the middle of the bush, stray domestic but now feral dogs - there being often no sight of a village or other human habitation nearby. Similarly one comes across donkeys, goats and cattle right out in the middle of nowhere – they are free to wander where they will – sometimes we come across these creatures fast asleep in the middle of the road and slow our vehicle to avoid an unpleasant accident. Had almost all the big cats not been hunted to extinction here they would not have gone short of food in the present day ...

My journal continues:

... after several fatiguing hours journey I have arrived at last in Janjanbureh [formerly Georgetown], the town on the island in the river where I am to serve my placement for at least the next year.

My Up-Country Home: closer to the Source.

In Francis Moore's day this island was called Lemain Island. At this time there was no settlement upon it. Moore tells us that it is:

... about four leagues in length on which are great numbers of beasts and palm trees which induces the natives to go often to ... [it] ... to hunt and draw palm wine ...

The British stationed troops here and eventually built Fort George on the north bank of the island in the early years of the nineteenth century to prevent any trade in slaves going down the river – this trade having been outlawed in 1807 across the British Empire. Georgetown grew up around the Fort and became a refuge for escaping slaves in the region

Writing in 1863, Sir Richard Burton, having just seen '... a sick officer ... half dead with fever from McCarthy's Island ...' describes it as '... This butt-end of the habitable world, a swamp six miles by four ...'

The settlement eventually became one of the largest and most important trading centres in the territory ... second only in size and importance to Bathurst [now Banjul]. Following Gambian independence in 1965 Georgetown's importance declined however with many business interests withdrawing due to a loss of business confidence. It was renamed **Janjanbureh** in the post-colonial period [variously spelt Janjanbureh, Janjangbureh and Jangjangbureh] though the names Georgetown and McCarthy [the latter name sometimes used for both the island and the settlement after Sir Charles McCarthy a former governor of Britain's West African territories] stubbornly persist.

The town itself stands or rather squats, on the northern most extremity of the island. Its low largely unremarkable buildings and other structures – some of which are of traditional construction with adobe walls and grass roofs – generally in substance and hue blend into the dirt roads that service them in a grid-iron pattern. The whole is homogenised further in the dry season by a layer of red dust and in the wet season by splashings of mud so that the overall impression is that the settlement is the dried out detritus left behind on a flood plain of the river after some great deluge and the water's recession. This earthen spectacle is sometimes broken up only by the green protrusions of mango, palm, baobab, cotton and other trees and vegetation that thankfully relieve its appearance here and there.

Main Street – Janjanbureh
(image courtesy of Radosław Botev)

My journal continues:

'There is a warm welcome from all my compound (*kunda*) family ... There are mainly women, girls and younger children to greet me - the men are not much in evidence. Apparently it is the womenfolk mainly who are to be found in any compound during the daytime hours - the men and older boys tend to be out until later. I am not to be introduced to Faa Bakary [meaning Father Bakary] yet. Our compound leader has in fact been away for some weeks now visiting his other wife at her compound somewhere back near the coast ...

Francis Moore reports in his 'Travels ...' that:

Every man is allowed to take as many wives as he pleases, some have no less than a hundred' and that he knew of '... a large town near Brucoe, in which are none but one man, his wives, children and slaves ...'

I discovered that things have changed since then and that these days there is a limit of four wives. The greater the number confers a greater status on the husband, it demonstrating that he has the greater wherewithal to support them.

I am pleasantly surprised by **my accommodation** on which **Mulai** from a nearby compound ... he is my landlord's son-in-law ... has been working for some time I am told. It is a small end of terrace one storeyed adobe house on the end of a line of four which stretch along the back perimeter wall of our compound. Internally there are two rooms, each approximately 10ft x10ft, one behind the other ... the walls have been freshly painted a bright cream - there is a flush loo and a shower in my own small walled yard situated through a back door out of my bedroom, so the rumours I heard on the coast about my special treatment have proved to be true. A flush loo and a shower are not standard VSO issue here and most of my colleagues have a pit latrine and a bucket and scoop. However sometimes, when the water demand is great, my loo and shower run dry ... in which case I resort to a bucket and scoop too as do my African neighbours at all times. Generally the water supply here is good and much better than back on the coast at my staging-post in Kanifing.

However other than my outside shower my house does not have its own running water and I must fetch it in jerry cans from the standpipe in the middle of the compound yard. Furthermore I must adapt to not having a sink or indeed any drainage inside my house. This means that you can't perform even the most basic functions in the normal way such as washing, teeth brushing, shaving or the washing of vegetables or dishes without devising a carefully worked out procedure. I have therefore become preoccupied with developing and learning practical strategies to be able to cope with a whole range of the most basic daily functions.

Without delay Mulai assists me in purchasing some African mater-ial at our local market for the making of door and window curtains – we take it straight to the tailor and they are to be ready within a few hours – this all for just a few pounds in English money from purchase of material to the finished articles. Similarly the two crude wooden and very uncomfortable easy chairs with which I have been issued need cushions. Mulai has a plan to source some foam and fabric for this purpose or to obtain some ready made chair seats at market but for such an elaborate need as this a trip to a much bigger market some 20 kilometres distance from my township will be necessary. If he fails to source this locally he may ask my compound head Faa Bakari to bring what I need back from the Kombos when he returns.

The all–purpose Mulai

My furniture is roughly made of cheap plywood – however many of the other houses in my compound have almost no furniture so I am lucky. As well as the 'easy' chairs I have a dining table or perhaps it's a kitchen table – I'm not sure. It is very high with two accompanying hard high dining chairs. There is a free standing cupboard/ sideboard with two drawers at the top. These drawers have no runners so that when they are half open they tip and fall out. The cupboard area below has no shelves so that it is hard to utilise the space efficiently.

In my bedroom there is unremarkably my bed which is a double. It has too few slats to support the thin foam mattress properly so that one has to be careful when lying on it to ensure that the support occurs where most needed. The mosquito net, which is suspended by strings fixed high up the two adjacent walls, covers the whole thing and has to be tucked in under the matress all the way around. It needs to be re-dipped in insect repellent every six months. The chest of drawers is made of the same rough plywood as the cupboard in the adjacent room and suffers from the same drawer tipping problems. I think it may have termite infestation because the contents of the drawers, namely my clothes, regularly become covered with a layer of fine sawdust.

Moore writes:

... My bed was raised from the ground about two feet ... I had a bed made of coarse cotton cloths, the produce of the country, which I got stuffed with silk-cotton a sort of down ... At the four corners ... I set up four poles to support a kind of pavilion made of thin cloth for keeping off the mosquitoes ... Other furniture, as I had little occasion for it, I was not troubled with it ...

I have decorated the wall facing my bed with an antique, ceremonial Mandinka mask which I purchased at the craft market in Fajara and brought up-country with me. It is said to bring good fortune and indeed to this point I feel things have gone well. But there is something about this mask which I can't yet quite comprehend or describe clearly. Its appearance expresses somehow the spirit, the deep culture of this place. It is inescapably African, not just in features but also in mood. But it contains too a suggestion of our universal primal core; in its silent stillness it says something about the forces, some dark, within which the elements of that core coalesced and evolved in this continental cradle of human kind. I feel that here one senses those fundamental and eternal constituents and the forces that shaped them; they run deep through this land and its people and go to the heart of us all.

I cover my bed with a blue and white African tie-dyed sheet also recently acquired but I can feel Africa around me so strongly that such small changes I can instigate add little.

Our African Beginnings: Anthropologists tell us that anatomically modern humans [AMH] first evolved in Africa approximately 200,000 years ago but around 100,000 years ago they were displaced in the Levant, the bridge to the rest of the world, probably through competition with Neanderthals and thus prevented from continuing the spread of their species towards global distribution. Around 60,000 years ago AMH's global distribution resumed. The period between the first incursion out of Africa and into the Levant which was halted and the second which succeeded in reaching lands beyond the Levant is known as **the African Interregnum**.[1] During this period Man is thought to have evolved his human consciousness in such a way as to make his global advance more achievable and ultimately more successful. It's as if the human psyche in essence had to be distilled and re-distilled in this African crucible before it could be released from this continent to find its global destiny.

In my kitchen/sitting room I have a fridge which runs of course only during those periods when the power supply is available. I also have a two ring gas burner powered by bottled gas. Along with the water filter these items are standard VSO issue. I am therefore able to make very passable porridge using powdered milk, oats, water and sugar though both the oats and the powdered milk are beyond the affordability of most of my African neighbours. The oats are in fact regarded with suspicion by my compound family not being the normal fare here. On the other hand I am constantly pestered by the compound children for my pow-

---

[1] as this goes to press I am told more recent research has moved its precise dates and duration

dered milk. They don't get nearly enough of this nor of any other milk to nourish their growth.

For the second time my landlady came to see me this morning to explain routines - this time concerning what to do with my empty jerry cans. As on the first occasion she was uncovered from the waist up. Given protocols back home this doesn't yet seem quite routine to me but as one of my female volunteer colleagues said when I mentioned this to her - 'Well you're just going to have to get used to it' ... and you know what - that's exactly what I'm doing.

I have been issued too with a new fan which needs to be assembled. I have already learnt on the coast just how vital a piece of the equipment this is - it is the difference between being able to sleep some of the time during the sweltering nights and not. Similarly there is a water filter which I have put into operation without delay. I have to filter water through it for several days however before what it produces becomes drinkable because the new filter leaves the water noxiously tainted. I am eternally grateful to the three fellow volunteers already in situ in my town, who are based in other compounds, for a supply of filtered water to tide me over until mine becomes drinkable.

I sleep under a net which has performed its task well and I don't seem to have had to share my small house with too much insect life so far ...

Slept well on my first night here and no insects have managed to penetrate my net except a cricket type creature ... The bites on my legs were I believe sustained at the local bar/restaurant which I attended last night with the other three volunteers who are currently based here ... I have got out of the habit of using my DEET repellent which perhaps was a bad idea ... there is a theory I have come across several times now that the insect life will direct its attention especially towards any newly arrived individual for whatever reason ...

I am still getting to know **my African family** and how they all relate to one another. This is made more difficult by the fact that sometimes when the women marry they change their family name and sometimes not. There is Ndella, Faa Bakari's senior wife [who, towards the end of my stay, I discovered was from royal Fulah stock], his daughters Fatou, Jainaba and Hawa ... then another Hawa who is a granddaughter as is Mama who is just 8 years old ... then a third Hawa who is a niece and her sister Efo and their brother Mohamed ... some are from the immediate family and some, the Bahs, from the extended family. This is all very confusing especially as everyone seems to be spoken of as a 'bruder' or 'seister'. Some children are here because they are looked after on a regular daily basis but don't belong to the family at all as blood relatives and don't usually sleep within our compound ... Will I ever learn who everyone is?

Fatou is heavily pregnant and will now speak of her unborn baby. Apparently one should never do this earlier on in a pregnancy as it is believed that this will bring bad luck.

The women in the compound are very industrious. They seem never to stop sweeping, cleaning, water-carrying, washing clothes, lighting fires, cooking, fumigating our rooms with incense having first stoked-up the incense-burner. They are up early each morning and soon busy themselves with pounding the rice for the morning's porridge in their great wooden mortars ... but also give high priority to sweeping the compound yard. This latter activity is a mystery to me ... the yard is littered with what looks to me like discarded rubbish such as rusty chairs, old cauldrons, pots and pans, piles of timber and of course the ever present chickens and goats wandering here and there scratching the largely bare earth to find anything they can to sustain them – but with palm frond brooms the younger females will sweep dust, soil and sand across the earthen yard from one side to another endlessly. True the soil surface will sometimes finish up with a regular pattern to it from the palm fronds and you think you have discovered the purpose of the task, to create a certain neatness, but then the sweeper will walk back across her own work even before the wind or any animal or other human traffic has itself had a chance to return the yard to its original state and you wonder what was the objective.

The men on the other hand seem to sit and benefit from all this activity. Often they will brew *ataya* - carefully going through the ritual of pouring this sweet green tea from teapot to glass cup and back again multiple times until foam forms on the surface of the liquid. Often the utensils for this process are provided by the women and taken away by them after use. When I asked my compound neighbour, Mohamed, about why the women seemed to work so hard and men just sit he said we work hard at other jobs and bring home the family income. Mohamed is a police inspector - but most men I come across seem to be unemployed. Employed or not this makes no difference to their contribution to the compound chores.

My family is very supportive, friendly and inquisitive ... especially the younger female members who spend a lot of time visiting my small house which is located at one end of the single-storey terrace of small houses which runs along the back wall of our compound. I suspect they find my behaviour unusual for a male as I spend quite a lot of my time in the compound. However I do not fully join in the life of the compound yard as they do but I always welcome their visits. They don't seem to mind my relatively more solitary habits and I suspect make allowances for me as some sort of exotic and more specifically as a *toubab*. I have just been offered some rice with dried fish and vegetables for breakfast ... it's not clear to me whether my tenancy includes food or not but I have been told by others that people here will always share their food in any event ... even when they don't have enough for themselves ... I have been made to feel very welcome here and my impression is that these people are truly decent, well-meaning, kind and generous.

Through Mulai I have agreed my monthly rent with my head of compound who is still absent as this year he has felt it right to celebrate *Koriteh* with his second wife. Apparently this arrangement includes all my washing and ironing but not the washing powder which I must buy myself.

Contrarily Moore reports that:
> ... it is usual as soon as a person arrives here to agree with some woman ... to wash their linen ... and with soap of their own making reckoned exceeding good.

Faa Bakari took his second wife when she was widowed by the death of one of his best friends. I am told her family have been very pleased with the arrangement which commits him to supporting her. With Mulai's help I have been able to confirm arrangements with and introduce myself to our compound head by phone. And guess what ... I have been renamed. I was warned on the coast that this would happen!

... the custom here is for the compound leader to give non-Africans joining a compound an African name. I think the practice is meant not just to give me a name that my African family know how to pronounce but to bestow acceptance and to initiate me into my *kunda* family as one of them. Of course it also implies the stripping away of the identity with which one arrives, the one that has been evolving all one's life which I'm sure on some level is the point. **I am to be known as Sariang Marong.** Faa Bakari has named me Sariang after his father and says I have therefore the role of his father - even though Faa Bakari is at least 10 years older than me. This is a great honour for me as the compound leader's father had a considerable reputation as a great hunter of game, especially leopards. He himself was given his name in honour of Sariang Kebbe, a prominent figure in the history of our township who was reputedly the first Gambian to do the Hajj on foot - it is said to have taken him three or four years journeying across the Sahara etc. Much of this earlier Sariang's life was therefore devoted to making progress in his spiritual journey. As an inheritor of the name of both of these men I feel I am in some sense expected to exhibit their strengths and achievements in some measure too but as I am neither a great hunter nor greatly travelled spiritually in my own opinion I find this a bit intimidating and wonder how I am going to live up to it.

Had I had the **hunting** skills of Faa Bakari's father and had I been happy to shoot leopards [which would have made me very unpopular in this day and age] I would have been very lucky to have got the opportunity to do so because there are now very few left in The Gambia [though numbers are unknown] and those that remain are elusive being nocturnal in habit. Perhaps Faa Bakari's father was largely responsible for this situation! There is some evidence that they remain however in small numbers north of the river in the coastal area in Niumi National Park. South of the river the last sighting was in in 2006 near Kyang West with occasional tracks having been found there since. The present situation contrasts with Henry F. Reeve's claim in *The Gambia: Its History* ... published in 1912 that leopards are very common indeed. Reeve also managed to see a lion though these are now not just nationally but also regionally extinct. Of some other big game species the same author tells us that the last trace of a giraffe was a carcass found in the vicinity of McCarthy Island, my island home, in 1899. Of the elephant Francis Moore says they '... generally go a hundred or two in a drove ...' but they are now extinct with the last elephant in The Gambia being shot in 1913. No doubt deforestation has played a role. Some estimates of the remaining hippos put the figure as low as 100 individuals although having seen a good number personally on a day long round-trip downstream from McCarthy Island this seems a bit low to me.

I have only been here a couple of days and a serious issue has arisen already ... I have broken my water filter. The filter 'candle' has fractured. I put out a call for the all-purpose Mulai who apparently will be here 'shortly' but this could mean almost any length of time so I sit it out ... a few hours later he arrives and his verdict is that no such replacement part can be obtained up-country and the matter will have to be referred to my own organisation's HQ back on the coast ...

One of our Hawas, Hawa Marong, took me to the market today to show me where to go, what there was and how to cope. The news of my new African name had gone before me and I was addressed as 'Sariang' or 'Sariang Marong' by all and sundry before I had a chance to introduce myself. The market here is almost exclusively for foodstuffs and hence is overwhelmingly staffed and attended by women with a few males staffing shops around the perimeter of the market e.g. a couple of tailors shops and a shoe shop. There is a marked **division of labour** here between the sexes. I am told that traditionally only women tend the rice fields for example - except for prisoners on work detail or on special unpaid labour days, instituted by the President, when even teachers or anyone else will leave their posts and go and work in the rice fields for no pay. Only men gather in the groundnut harvest.

Moore:

...The men work the corn ground and the women and girls the rice ground ...' and later of the women '... in regard to the fowls ... they breed [them] up in great quantities ...

We walked up and down the rows of stalls - not stalls really but rather pitches on the ground - with their meagre offerings - fly blown meat of indistinguishable variety and fish [mainly the ubiquitous Bonga which I soon discovered contained so many tiny bones as to be difficult to negotiate], fruit and vegetables often split and bruised that would never have left the farm back in the UK. At every turn the ladies invited me to patronise their stall - smiling their broad smiles up at me from their seated position on the ground exposing their missing and rotten teeth. You wondered how they could possibly scratch any sort of a living out of this. You wondered too what you could find to take back home to produce something at least edible if not appetising on your regulation VSO two ring gas hob.

10.09.2010 ... Today is *Koriteh* their name for Eid at the end of Ramadan [of it Moore says: '... *When the moon is expired they make a great feast at which they kill abundance of cows and are very merry ...*'] and I have been presented with my first set of African clothes by my compound family so that I can be dressed properly for this festival during which **I am to be presented to the town Chief [*Sefo*] and other town worthies** ... These clothes are a gift from my 'son' Faa Bakari, my compound head and they consist of baggy pantaloons which are gathered at the ankles and a collarless smock with long slanted and pointed sleeves which reach down to my shins ... This all in dark blue with pale blue/almost white tiny characters arranged in repeating lines covering the whole except for the ankles and cuffs. I think it is splendid and wish my family and friends back in the UK could see me in it but with such poor internet links there is little chance of relaying an electronic image to them.

The author in his first set of African clothes – a gift from Faa Bakari

A meeting with the town chief was scheduled for 10.30 this morning ... my fellow volunteers from Mulai's compound, namely Bakari [Pete] and Hawa [Liz] are also coming ... In the event I might have guessed that we would be running on Gambian time and did not leave for the meeting with the chief until 1pm ... By the time we arrived at the chief's compound we were advised that he was taking a nap and so our meeting has been postponed until 5.30pm ... which could mean any time this evening ...

In the interim we did meet Councillor Ebrima Foon [if I caught his name correctly] at his house. He was very welcoming. We sat talking to him and his wife, Hawa [another one!!] ... who lolled on the sofa next to him with their toddler son Bundu whilst a recording of a famous Senegalese musician played through the TV set speakers ... Afterwards Mulai, Bakari and I had a group photograph taken ... all in our African clothes with Mulai still wearing his non-traditional baseball cap as he did in most circumstances ...

[I frequently came across this strange mixture of the old and new, the ceremonial and the formal with the unreservedly practical. These incongruities seem to go unnoticed by my African colleagues and neighbours. Indeed a senior education officer colleague with whom I shared an office, namely Amat Bah, would regularly wear a child's cowboy hat. This was for a period his most favoured mode of head cover whether he was delivering a formal address at a school prize day or greeting senior VIP visitors ... though he would revert to an Islamic pill-box cap or takiyah sometimes and particularly on Fridays whence colleagues repaired en masse to the town's central mosque for the early afternoon call to prayer.]

In the evening my compound family dressed in their finest and took a bowl of food and some money to the compound gate where, as tradition dictates, they distributed these to passers-by especially those adjudged in greatest need. I should pause here to mention the girls' dresses in more detail. What a range of bright colours, head scarves etc. The little girls were as bright as the older girls and women - they included two sisters in matching dresses in glittering gold, one of our Hawas in a lilac jacket and shirt, the latter went down to the ground and a yellow head scarf. Little Mariam (Mama) has some special beaded hair braids with a blue and gold outfit.

It was a great shame that a downpour had them in full retreat scurrying back to the compound veranda at which time I was pleased to have the opportunity to contribute to the funds for distribution. Thankfully the rain soon stopped and the distribution continued. Giving to others in this way, in accordance with Islamic principles, is here inculcated from early childhood I am told ...

Indeed I have noticed that Gambians are generous always. They will never eat in front of anyone without offering to share - even when they have precious little for themselves. One will often have to refuse firmly to discourage their continuing offers.

Our meeting with the chief finally took place at about 7pm as darkness was falling very suddenly after sunset - as it tends to here. Not sure what I had been expecting but the Chief's compound with various buildings and houses including his own house seemed just as ramshackle as everyone else's. By the time we arrived the national flag at the gate had been lowered for the day as it was apparently every day around this time. We were shown to the Chief's unlit veranda by another compound resident and I was given pride of place in a chair set in front of my colleagues who sat on the benches behind me. The chief came out to us through a doorway from a lit room and took his seat with his back to this door. It was therefore impossible to see his face even though he sat just a couple of feet in front of our group. This was disconcerting to say the least because at no point during our meeting was I able to see the chief's face though I was aware that mine must have been fully visible to him. His outline however gave a sense of his bulk which was not inconsiderable. Initial pleasantries being exchanged I expressed what a great honour it was to meet him. As I listened to him my facial expressions in response to what he said must have looked very artificial in the absence of any facial prompts or other visual clues from him that would elicit them naturally. As I sat listening to the tones of his disembodied voice filling the heavy evening air on the veranda I formed the impression of a kindly and relaxed leader of no inconsiderable charm. He seemed to command the respect of the local fellow Africans who for one reason or another came and went for various reasons interrupting our meeting as they did so. Later I was told by Mulai that although the Chief had inherited his position from his father upon his death it still required confirmation by the general endorsement of the populous of our town which had been freely given.

Our exchanges were a little perfunctory at times though pleasant ... the chief welcomed me with some formality to the town. I expressed a satisfaction with having come to reside here for a period and looked forward to the experience. I did learn that the Chief had come from a Mandinka father and a Fulah mother. Before too long our small group took its leave of the Chief but not before each of us had presented him with a 50 dalasi note. This was in lieu of and apparently a perfectly acceptable alternative to, the kola nuts which Mulai informed us belatedly etiquette demanded we should have taken to him as a gift.

I left with the uncomfortable feeling that should I subsequently meet the Chief in the street, which almost certainly I would at some point soon, I would not be able to acknowledge his presence and say hello as I would be unable to recognise him.

The meeting over we adjourned to a local bar for beer with a couple of other volunteers as pre-arranged [not, that is, before Mulai had taken his leave – in fact with one or two exceptions our African friends, colleagues and acquaintances never drank alcohol with us and did not frequent such places] and thence on to dinner with some volunteers at their house situated in Mulai's compound.

My journal continues:

... the deficiencies in infrastructure and the essentials of life here are more than made up for by the generosity and spirit of the people. There is a warm welcome from all you meet, genuine offers of assistance, the solid support of your *kunda* family which takes you in as one of its own without reserve, the smiling faces of the children, the dignity and resourcefulness of those in hardship and the mutual respect they show towards one another and towards a stranger ... the optimism for the future ... always and **everywhere the Paraclete** ... there is so often the most brilliant light in this traditionally so-called 'Dark Continent'.

Having at last reached what will be my home for some considerable time and having begun to settle in I feel I can sit back to reflect on my new surroundings; to feel them atmospherically; to breathe in fully a sense of place. I sit in the afternoon at one end of the veranda in my compound at the door to my small adobe house and take in **the timelessness of it all**. One is presented with a scene that can't have changed much for hundreds, perhaps thousands of years. The floppy eared sheep push open the entrance gate with their noses when they arrive from the Darbo *kunda* – some distance away in the town, their other home – a compound containing some of our extended family. They know they belong here but also there in the other compound and manage to travel between the two unshepherded. My compound people chatter on reassuringly to one another as they sit in the shade. As an observer who understands nothing of what they say one can nevertheless tell that the content is less important than the fact that the chatter occurs and occurs incessantly. The unforgiving heat bears down and the crickets keep up their unfaltering electric monotone. The call to prayer echoes through the air, through the majestic baobabs and cotton trees with their flocks of weaver birds. The chickens scratch in the red earth. All this somehow speaks of a deep continuity but also of something which is intangible, indomitable, pulsing, and ubiquitous ... .a force which carries magic and mystery that cannot be fully described or understood but only felt - something which is special to this continent and its people.

What is strange about my new situation is that before I came here I prepared myself psychologically to be alone. I expected to be a stranger in a land that I would not understand and that would not understand me ... and in some sense I was looking forward to it. I was looking forward to having my own thoughts uninterruptedly for a prolonged period to see where they would take me. Yet I seem to have become transplanted into a compound life where I feel I am valued and cared for in spite of my preparedness for self-containment and what-do-you-know - I don't mind. The power of human beings to coalesce as social animals, even when so many cultural and practical differences might have intervened adversely to inhibit this and in spite of themselves is remarkable.

The rain is drumming on my roof again having been preceded by the usual powerful squall that rattles all before it. It is drumming and drumming above me reassuringly as it has done so often since my arrival in West Africa.

The wind comes first and blows excessive hard for the space of half an hour before any rain falls ...
writes Francis Moore

To Work

Monday and my work as management advisor to the **Central River Region Education Directorate** commenced today. I rose at about 7am this morning but the heat of yesterday had lingered even more so than usual in view of a further power failure yesterday - this time the problem was within our compound and not the area supply. This meant the fans were inactive all last evening as well as in the early hours of this morning when they would normally have run through until 2am. By the time I have expended the minimal energy needed to shave, shower, brush my teeth and to get dressed I had already broken into a sweat and this before undertaking the 10 to 15 minute walk along the couple of dirt roads to my place of work. I am naturally a brisk walker but here you have to remember to walk slowly to avoid over-heating.

The direct route takes me past the prison, the local authority headquarters and **Armitage Senior Secondary School** which is one of the most prestigious schools in the country though modest by western standards.

The Regional Education Directorate occupies a group of office, residential and other buildings spread out on a site of perhaps a couple of acres on the north side of a dirt road that runs from the edge of my township to the western extremity of the island. The initial impression is of a tidily arranged and well-kept campus with solidly built infrastructure but a closer inspection shows that this is not so. Nothing seems to be built to a sufficiently high standard or quality to last. I had been told that there had been a general refurbishment within the last few months and that the buildings had been officially re-opened with a great fanfare. Already however there are signs of deterioration – for example most of the doors don't fit their frames properly. This is perhaps more an issue of cheap materials than workmanship though both leave much to be desired. We in the West should not feel superior about this. In countries like this such a state of affairs is simply a consequence of the lack of resources and finance which results in the non-availability of better raw materials and better trained staff who have the right tools to execute the work. The deterioration is also a function of the extreme climatic conditions – particularly the intense heat during the hot season and the intense humidity and wetness during the wet season. The lavatory areas on the end of the blocks which had figured in the general upgrade gave the impression of dilapidation and neglect that would normally in Northern Europe take decades to accrue.

On my arrival at the gate to the education directorate compound I could see several individuals, including a couple of my fellow volunteers, studying some notices pinned up along the outside wall of one of the office blocks. After making enquiries about this I was told that most of those studying the notices were teachers wanting to know who had been posted to their schools for this year.

Building containing my office at the Central River Region Education Directorate – Janjanbureh

I learned later that all postings are reviewed nationally on a yearly basis and that on average 20 per cent of teachers, head teachers and deputies are moved to fresh locations/schools. Further postings are not announced until shortly [a few weeks] before the commencement of the school year in which they take effect and prompt a flurry of activity related to moving to the new location. There is much special pleading by individuals to get decisions changed. Formerly the more remote rural, up-country locations were avoided by many staff who would do whatever it took to be less off the beaten track. Now an allowance system has been devised within the pay structure to create financial incentives for unpopular postings and often the reverse will happen, namely that there is competition for them.

It is not uncommon however for those particularly unhappy with the outcome of the posting exercise to leave the profession and take up alternative employment if they can get it or even to revert to unemployment.

My journal continues:

> I deposit myself in an office which had not been allocated to me because no arrangements for my or anyone else's arrival seems to have been made. A new regional director has been posted here but the handover date seems uncertain, it now having been postponed from tomorrow or the day after [no one seems quite sure of the original date] to Friday ... we think!
>
> At 9am, following the schedule that pertains for the part of the town where this office is located, the power supply comes on and I attempt to get online. I manage this only intermittently with a connection-speed painfully slow when extant.
>
> It may be of interest to note that those of my colleagues who were around spent most of their time talking in groups outside their offices away from their desks and computers. [note: it took me some time to realise that a colleague sitting at a computer was just as likely to be thought by his/her colleagues to be at play rather than at work and conversely that talking outside the office is just as likely to be construed as work than as relaxing socially or time-wasting. This was just the way of things there]. I soon joined my colleagues to exchange pleasantries and to find out what I could about work. 'Laid-back' hardly captures strongly enough the tenor of the ethos.
>
> Eventually after a morning spent with little to occupy me of a work nature I decided to walk back to my compound to check on progress with the electrical fault. On my way there I noticed a donkey just standing still with head down, not

eating, eyes frequently closing. It looked exhausted and I thought decidedly ill. Its tether was not secured to anything leaving it completely free to roam but it chose not to move.

At my compound I found the all-purpose Mulai - he explained that the electricians had re-established our supply. The girls brought me lunch - rice of course with a small amount of chicken and vegetables. I ate this gratefully and languidly before my return to the regional directorate. On my way I passed the donkey once more - it had hardly moved. I stopped to look at it but was distracted by someone a short distance from me and glanced away. When I looked back a matter of seconds later **the donkey** had **keeled over** and looked close to death. I asked the person nearby what he thought about the donkey in case its plight had gone unnoticed. With no apparent concern he said 'I don't know - perhaps it's dying'. His indifference was shared by the other Africans loitering in the vicinity and by those passing by. I continued my journey back to work and thought of Auden's poem 'Musee Des Beaux Arts' and Brueghel's painting 'Landscape with the Fall of Icarus' and what they say about the potential for our indifference in the face of calamity for other living beings - human or otherwise.

On reaching work I discovered that an area power-cut had left the office without a supply. Soon, in desultory fashion, most colleagues melted away for the day and I followed suit. I hoped this wasn't going to be a typical day in my life at the Directorate.

Second day at work and though the power supply has been restored there is no internet connection. This continued until 11am after which it was restored but only falteringly. I took the opportunity to perform an internet banking transaction that was urgently needed to keep my finances in good order but the link was so weak that every time I tried to do this I was timed-out and eventually gave up. Given the poor telephone network connections I could not perform the relevant account transaction by phone either and the matter remained unresolved. In terms of work there is still no sign of the new regional director, no one to assist in my integration into the work to be done and indeed not much sign of work or progress on anyone's part on anything.

In lieu of any directives from anyone regarding my role I have arranged a series of meetings, initially with my senior colleagues, to establish what they do so that I can consider how I might be able to give support.

19.09.2010: Today is Sunday and having been on standby at work all day yesterday and today for a possible meeting of all directorate staff with our new regional director, I was called at very short notice to a meeting this afternoon at approximately 4pm. This was a brief welcoming meeting at which everyone was asked to introduce themselves but when it came to my turn the outgoing regional director introduced me to his successor himself. I think this was somehow meant as a mark of my status through age, experience, position – but I am not sure. The incoming regional director is very mildly spoken but with an assertive handshake. I know this because at the end of the meeting I took the trouble to shake his hand and said that I was looking forward to working with him. He returned the compliment. The formal handover meeting from the old to the new Regional Director is scheduled for tomorrow at 8.30am and is expected to last a couple of hours.

When I arrived back at my *kunda* (compound), the **arrival of the head of our compound** had occurred as scheduled and we greeted one another graciously. I must say that I have taken an immediate liking to him. He is very charming and relaxed and carries authority, though my initial impression is that the women are the dominant force in this family. Faa Bakari, our head, has kindly remembered to bring back with him from the coast the foam seat cushions I needed for my easy chairs and the new water filter 'candle' to replace the one I broke which he picked up from my NGO's HQ. He also presented me with some incense sticks as a gift. The womenfolk must have told him during a phone call whilst he was away that I had commented on how much I enjoyed their censing of my rooms using their large incense burner. I thought this a most thoughtful touch on the part of all concerned.

My precise role will I think be an evolving one ... I am officially management advisor to the Regional Director, the senior and other education officers of the Directorate and the head teachers of the Central River Region. Our regional directorate is one of six nationally.

... My initial impression is that the policies and procedures that have been adopted here are very sound, comprehensive and well thought through. They have been created with the support of the VSO, the American Peace Corps and several other NGOs. There are a number of Scandinavian organisations operating here which have a very good reputation for their contributions to the education sector amongst others. The main issue here seems to be implementation of these policies and procedures on the ground at service delivery and both the Director and I hope that this is where I may be able to hand on some management strategies/methods that will help and prove sustainable. There will be a big challenge in adapting what I have learnt in the UK to a cultural context that is so different and I can see already that I have much more to learn than I have to pass on ...

My People, their Lives and their Circumstances

14.09.10 ... The heat has been intense again today. After work instead of going the shortest route home I took a short detour to the north ferry point and then back home via our township's main street. This was perhaps a 20 minute walk, perhaps less. The centre of the town covers a very small area. I managed to buy a dozen lollipops at 1 dalasi each for my compound children en route. By the time I got home I was drenched in sweat. The sun here really is unforgiving. It took coming to West Africa for me to realise that one can actually sweat at the knees ... yes great patches of moisture coming through my thin trousers. The lollipops were well received!

... have now been up country for over 3 weeks ... a very bad evening for insects last night ... they are hard to ignore ... the floor of my house this morning is littered with the hundreds of bodies of those that have been sprayed, squashed, burnt by flying into the light bulb etc ... all shapes and sizes up to 3 inches ...

This evening **the younger females in the compound** came to see me to ask questions about myself and where I come from. Like young people back home or anywhere else they have excitement about the future and ambitions for themselves. Jainaba is 23, Hawa 19, another Hawa 16, yet another Hawa 14 and Mama 8. They asked about London and what it is like, about whether there are any Muslims there. They shared a common aim to get married and move to the Kombos [muni-cipal districts in the west of the country around the coastal area and Banjul the capital]. How this fits in with their other ambitions I do not know. Jainaba wants to travel to see much more of the world and 19 year old Hawa likes India and Indian fashion and wants to visit that country. I could not help but wonder to myself how realistic some of these ambitions might be given the relative poverty of even the better-off people here in global terms and considering the cost of travel etc. I also learnt that Jainaba had spent most of the day in bed due to a bout of malaria. She says this is the third time she has had it. I gave her one of my stock of anti-malarial capsules which she seemed to appreciate. I know that they are used in the treatment as well as the prevention of the disease but of course she really needs a full course which I can't supply. Many of the Africans to whom I have spoken claim a history of malaria and often don't seem to regard it as of any great consequence.

The girls also explained to me some of the marriage practices here. I was told that the typical age varies from tribe to

Mama Marong

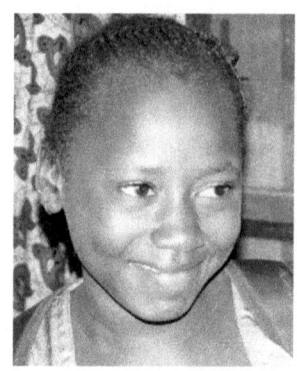
Efo Bah

Hawa Jallow

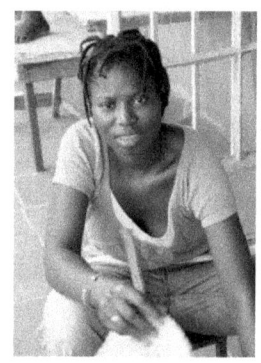
Hawa Bah

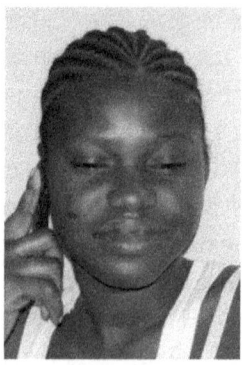
Hawa Marong

Sibo posing for the camera and playing it cool

tribe – amongst the Mandinka [my own compound family is mainly Mandinka] they said it is usually between 15 and 20 years old whereas for some tribes it can be as low as between 10 or 12. One of the Hawas was explaining that she won't be allowed to pick her own husband – her parents will do that – but she will be allowed to say no if she really objects. Also if they run out of ideas she may suggest names of potential husbands herself but they may be rejected out of hand. She said she will not be allowed to be on her own with her prospective husband until after they are married.

Through our conversation I became aware of how starkly **my culture and theirs** differs but also that there is an appreciation of this on both sides, a strong urge to explore the other's world and preparedness to make allowances for misunderstandings and unintended offence. There is a generosity here which is pure gold and unmistakable in any culture. During our discussion at one point a small cicada appeared on my floor in our midst. Our group's generosity didn't quite stretch to it and unhesitatingly and unremarked our 16 year old Hawa moved her leg forward and squashed it with her bare foot. Its remains were cleared away tidily before the girls left to return to their own houses in our compound.

Just after leaving, the oldest Hawa came back with a bowl of salt water. She sprinkled it on the veranda just outside my door and explained that this would discourage the many frogs that had appeared as a result of the latest bout of rain. They had been threatening to enter my doorway for much of the evening being attracted by the insects which were themselves attracted by my light. The salt water had an immediate effect with frogs beating a hasty retreat off the veranda back to the darkness of the compound yard.

Recording his findings in the 1730s on the subject of early marriage Moore writes:

... They give away their daughters when they are young, some as soon as they are born and the parents never after-

> wards break the match ... she [the betrothed] cannot ... nay dares not marry any other. They [husbands] take their wives ... before they do so they are obliged to pay the parents of the wife two cows, two iron bars and two hundred cola, a fruit that comes a vast way inland ...

I can report that payments and the cola nut traditions are still alive and well in The Gambia.

Today is Saturday and the eldest Hawa has taken me to watch **a local football match** with her. Hawa is an imposing young woman in her carefully chosen clothes which are almost always traditionally African – and her head is usually covered with a cala [Mandinka name for a hijab]. One young male acquaintance of hers to whom she introduced me proclaimed of her 'She is a lioness!' which I assumed to be local parlance and high praise indeed. There have however been no lions here for some time. There is no doubt that Hawa has a great deal of self-possession.

One of the football teams in the game we were watching had an African place name which I couldn't quite catch; the other was called 'Manchester United' – the original in the UK being a much supported club side here. I notice too that there are many local youths sporting replica England football shirts. England seems to be the most supported national team. The Gambia is too of course but isn't much mentioned. On the surface at least there seems to be no residual post-colonial resentment and sometimes a hint that The Gambia is lucky to have had **the British connection** rather than the French connection like their close neighbour Senegal and many of the other West African nations. This must be an issue of identity for in many ways they share our outlook. Like most of us, Gambians want to be who they are and not someone else. But in many ways they have precious little to thank us for from their 400 year association with England and subsequently the British Empire. In terms of infrastructure there seems to me to be little or nothing worthy of note left behind from the colonial period.

It is early October and the wet season continues. For much of last evening and throughout the night we had torrential rain and thunderstorms – indeed this has been the pattern for several days now and I am told that it has been known to rain for a week without stopping. In the night when the rain does subside periodically and the drumming on my corrugated roof ['the corrugate'] ceases, the sound of the cicadas bleeds through the air like a drone to occupy the vacated auditory space. It reminds me of the characteristic base line accompaniment of a piece of medieval music from a hurdy-gurdy with its unchanging, unremitting tone. Whenever there is no rain at night the cicadas are with us, as they are during the day. It's as if they can't bear to miss a moment of 'on air' time.

This morning when I got up the downpour had reduced to a medium drizzle. There were tiny frogs moving to and fro on the veranda outside my door, sometimes jumping at lightning speed to cover the next foot or so of their journey. The rain had darkened the red earth in our compound yard leaving puddles and potholes everywhere. These will be made larger by the traffic of people, the occasional visit of a donkey drawn carts or even of a motorised vehicle as the day goes on.

The land here up-country in the wet season has to be seen for one to understand the problems of movement created. The scarred earth scored often so deeply with ruts between areas of swamp, mud and potholes ... .all contribute to this and progress can be very slow or sometimes totally impossible.

At this time of year there is a constant battle to keep oneself and one's clothes clean and fresh. When it is hot the humidity is often intense – even though a little less so here up-country than back on the coast – and one breaks into a sweat at the slightest exertion. Also one's trousers become spattered in red mud from the huge puddles and potholes to be found in the unmade-up roads and indeed everywhere else. This is unavoidable no matter how carefully one treads. It sometimes makes you feel as if Man wasn't meant to be here fighting a constant and often losing battle against the elements - as if our occupancy here in Africa is only temporary and unnatural.

The nights here draw in very quickly and there is little in the way of street lighting. It is always wise to carry a torch after dark to check what one is stepping on, though few Africans seem to bother and I more often than not forget ... I always worry about treading on the frogs that abound on wet nights - some are tiny.

Moore records that:

... what seemed to me strange at first was that as soon as it grows light the sun rises and as soon as it sets it gets dark ... He goes on to tell us that he got so used to this whilst in Africa that when he went back to England ... *being sometimes a good way from home I had a fear of being benighted and made what haste I could and have often been there [home] an hour before it grew dark.*

The River at Sunset

The bird life here is truly exotic. I have never seen such a range of vividly coloured and liberally plumed specimens - points of brilliance against a backdrop of a more conservative hue. There are beautiful metallic blues shading into black and most spectacularly some of the brightest reds with black and white and there are green parakeets too. Remarkably some of the insect life can almost compete with this ornithological display.

The call to prayer is the never failing, the unremitting vocal metronome which marks the passing of our day. It seems to have been intensified in volume for Ramadan. I wake at around 5am as it blasts its way across the township. It is insistent and unrelenting at this time and seems devoid of the beauty of intonation that can make it so appealing. No concessions are made to those who may need rest; not even to the seriously ill or dying.

As Ramadan comes to an end the teapots re-appear and the ritual of **brewing of** *ataya*, the sweet green tea so popular with the men especially, resumes. The brewing of *ataya* is held by many to be a somewhat disreputable activity - I think it is associated with relaxation, time wasting and being too laid-back [though how one distinguishes between that and the normal pace of life I don't quite see] - but it also serves a social bonding function. The tea is made with huge amounts of sugar and is tipped backwards and forwards from glass to teapot many times creating a thin foam on its surface. To accept a glass of this sometimes almost viscous liquid is to accept the brotherhood of the group and the gift of the craftsmanship and loving care with which it has been made.

... The power cuts here are mainly scheduled ones - 2am to 9am and 4pm to 7pm. This is a great improvement on the Kombos where we rarely ate dinner from beginning to end without being plunged into darkness without warning... but then this is the wet season.

... already there is a request from my NGO for me and the other new volunteers to return to the coast to arrange for some essential documentation that we don't yet have including my biometric ID... That means a 3 day trip at least... some of which is quite gruelling.

A Trip to the Coast and a Glimpse of the Journey

... Left my compound early for the ferry crossing point when the day was young, fresh and quiet. In no time I had reached the river which is always so magnificent it takes your breath away. The River Gambia, as you might expect, is simply referred to as 'the River'. It dominates this small country from end to end and yet in the present age – unlike in times gone by when trade in slaves, gold, ivory and much more was flourishing – it carries very little traffic. In the early morning, before the heat of the day gets up, you can see it cloaked in a rising and gently swirling mist looking as if it is the original primal swamp from which all life has come. Not unusually too, as *this* morning, you will see the occasional dugout canoe with its solitary boatman, an early fisherman modestly plying his way along the river. In relative scale the man and the river confirm the true might of this arterial, life giving splendour and what must have been its huge impact on land and Man down the ages. The mist hugs the landscape, it hugs the bush, blurs the place at which land and sky, river and sky meet and as he recedes into the distance the solitary canoeist becomes a mere reference point witnessed by the brooding bush, by the graceful palms lining the river's banks and through the special privilege bestowed by this early hour before the interference of more intense human commerce, by you.

... eventually enough early travellers had gathered for it to be worthwhile for one of the small ferry boats, who offer a service at an extra charge before the main and larger ferry starts running, to take us to the other bank and I managed to catch the regular green bus bound for the Kombos. It had no less than three live goats lashed to the roof... I endured most of the 10 hour journey with a chicken sitting on my left foot.

It belonged to the lady with the wonderfully wide hips with whom I shared a double seat which was really only wide enough for one and a half people of normal size anyway. Many things are very different here and I haven't seen most of them before ... not even in Willsden ... not even on the High Road.

And then the girl with the straightened hair sitting at the front, whose eye I caught accidentally - fixing her gaze on me - leaving the bus when it stopped on the ferry to come around outside the bus to where I was sitting on the inside ... she tapping on my window quite blatantly to attract my attention ...

During my few days of business on the coast I stayed at Mama's, a hotel and restaurant down a dirt track in Fajara off the Bakau Road some 20 minutes' walk from our NGO HQ office. There was a warm welcome from Mama herself, a weathered and time-worn German speaking Swiss. On the first evening I met with 8 or 10 volunteers for dinner. Torrential downpour again ... the frogs came out in force. Before retiring to bed I finished up sharing a late night drink with a Stuttgart German who in the course of our discussion demonstrated he had been here long enough to want to complain about almost everything Gambian.

24.09.10 ... following up on a tip-off from a fellow volunteer I left the coast a day or two earlier than planned as I was able to get a lift back up-country with a group of members from the Gambian National Assembly, including the Deputy Speaker and other luminaries. They were **fact-finding** for one **select committee** project report or another. The *gelleh-gelleh* in which we travelled hired for their exclusive use was rickety, had no internal upholstery except some on the seats which had springs coming through them, windows which didn't work properly, cracks in the windscreen and sparks flying off the battery under the driver's seat. There was what felt like virtually no suspension. The roof inside was covered with signs of post-manufacture spot welding with metal plates etc. that had been added into the superstructure for reasons now entirely unclear. Everything rattled .There wouldn't be the remotest chance that this vehicle would pass the MOT back in the UK.

As VIPS we were waved straight through at the Barra Ferry which apparently could so often be a bottle neck, but not before an Imam climbed into our vehicle to say a prayer for the success of the fact-finding mission and for our safe deliverance from it. Each member of our party faced towards him with arms outstretched, palms upturned and heads bowed, chanting in response to his litany. This culminated in a final appeal to Allah at which point each participant tapped his forehead lightly with their fingertips. After the Imam had accepted some small monetary offerings he left us as quickly as he had come.

En route up-country at the various police and army check-points, of which there are an absurd number in such a small country, the initially assertive and sometimes aggressive guards would instantly stand to attention and apologise for themselves, as soon as they realised who my travelling companions were. At one point one of the assembly members who had been a teacher, prior to his election to the National Assembly, ticked-off one of his former students, now a soldier, who had failed to identify him initially - saying to him, 'You still owe me that essay on such and such ... ' amidst hoots of laughter from all in our party ... it's a small country.

Eventually and unsurprisingly our vehicle broke down in a remote part of the bush as light was fading. The problem related to the sparks coming off the battery under the driver's seat. We all left the *gelleh-gelleh* to stretch our legs. I witnessed a beautiful sunset to the accompaniment of the cicada chorus. As I gazed back along the road down which we had travelled which ran due west to the coast - a spectacular kaleidoscope of light effects and colours beamed towards us

– with dappled red and yellow pockets arranged finger-like reaching out to the landscape in an arc.

The driver and his 'conductor' managed to get us going again after about 30 minutes and we continued on what was for me the last leg of my journey. By now it was getting late and I knew that for our party to reach my island home and their first day's stop-over, we would have to re-cross the river from the north bank to the island. When we reached the ferry point, as some had forecast, the ferry had stopped running for the day but the VIP status of the group was again brought into play, to re-commission it for an additional, late crossing. Eventually we reached my township where Assembly members had been invited to dinner by the Regional Governor which invitation was extended to me. I declined politely as I knew my *kunda* family was expecting me and had saved some food for me ... they had tracked my progress periodically by an exchange of texts. We had by then journeyed less than 180 miles up-country in 9.5 hours of bone-shaking travel since we left Banjul and I had learnt that there is a lot of making-do for everyone here no matter who you are ... but also much use of and respect for status and position.

... it is late and I am ensconced in my bed under my net ... the rain has started up and is drumming with real force on my roof, as it has done time and time again since I arrived here in West Africa. I am thankful for the respite it brings from the insects and for cooling down the long hot day.

I drift to sleep beneath the gaze of the ceremonial Mandinka mask on my bedroom wall ... I feel its safe presence ... it presides steadfastly, serenely but enigmatically over my sleeping hours and offers a portal to and protection through those other realms wherein lie the deep mysteries of Africa, of the magnificent river with its peace and silences, of the true nature of ourselves, our pasts and futures, of **our human journey** and of life itself. Through the penumbra of sleep I can see again the solitary canoeist in his craft who comes from nowhere we know and goes to somewhere which we can only glimpse in moments of truth. He plies his way downstream into the dense early morning mist in the distance until his image breaks up and he becomes absorbed into the infinite landscape beyond. And I am left with only the memory of him, as we are of others who have passed through our lives, our lost fathers and mothers, our lost brothers and grandfathers, our lost friends and our lost lovers, who inhabit the world that has claimed him too. And there is just silence, a receding sense of self, the mask and eternity and the never ending river and peace ... and a sense of wonder and of the Journey and of the privilege of witness ...

Back Up-Country

Now it was late September and though the tourist season would not be upon us fully, until the wet season had left us in another couple of weeks, the township's outlying safari camps were already beginning to receive their first tour parties.

I went with a volunteer colleague – re-named Sankumba – to take **dinner and a few beers at the nearest camp just across the river** from our township. Responding to our phone call the camp sent a small boat to pick us up and take us over. We returned late into the evening when daylight had gone and the river was very high from the rains. We had to wade ashore for the final few yards because the river had overflowed its banks and our boat ran aground before we reached its new margin. We paddled ashore at a point further upriver than the usual landing place, a point unused to disembarkation and human traffic.

My unrevised staccato notes read thus:

> Echoing impressions – the banks in silhouette, the German travel party, the candle powered and hurricane lamps, the empty and immense breadth of the river, its blurred and distant banks, the lateness of the hour, the lapping of the water against our hull, the greys of varying intensity that form the landscape after nightfall under an almost full

moon, the shrieks of the nocturnal creatures as we cross the mighty river fly through the air over our heads and echo back from the distant bank underlining the pervading silence in mid-stream where nothing moves except us ... quietly ... with only the low throbbing of our engine. My silent prayers for our safe return to the already sleeping town, our wading through the shallows and the blindness of our footing beneath the water's surface amidst whatever lurks there; the lush vegetation of the bank at the now arbitrary new water margin unused to human footfall.

29.09.10 ... This is the third bad day for **insects** in the evening, which at least one NGO colleague back on the coast had told me to expect in my placement destination. When the climatic conditions are optimally conducive for them they appear and have been particularly numerous between 9pm and 11pm. All manner of insects find their way through cracks and the narrowest gaps at the edges of fly screens, under and around door frames. They are difficult to ignore. I take out as many as I can ... some are large, several inches and others tiny. They include spiders, crickets, cockroaches and a very large flying beetle, as well as myriads of what back home we might describe as gnats and of course mosquitos. By the time the invasion is slowing down the floor of my sitting room come kitchen is littered with their bodies. The girls have advised me too, which advice I have followed, to put a large bowl of water under my light so that as the insects collide with the light they are stunned by its heat and plummet out of the air into the bowl below where they drown. It seems quite effective.

30.09.10 ... at last an opportunity to meet **the Regional Director** on a one-to-one basis and I felt this was a good start to what I hope will be a productive relationship. Learnt much about his background and family circumstances ... he has a daughter and son-in-law in London and plans to go there next Christmas. He says he wants support in creating a team approach and would like input on management techniques. He would like to introduce me to local head teachers himself. He knows that madrassas in our care need many more visits than they are getting currently and that the school management manual needs to be better implemented.

04.10.10 ... It continues to be very hot, often uncomfortably so, as we are not yet out of the wet season. The humidity levels are very high and whenever there is power my electric fan is in constant use. At night I fall asleep with the fan oscillating across one side of my mosquito net. When the power goes off as scheduled at 2am the heat builds once more until it wakes me up in a pool of sweat usually between 2.30 and 3am. I try to feign sleep to myself as well as I can until the temperature drops of its own accord between about 4 and 5am. This allows another hour, maybe two, of real sleep before this becomes no longer possible between 6 and 7 when the sun begins to climb once more up high into the sky.

My township has **one of the oldest churches in West Africa** - perhaps the oldest. It is a Methodist church. At last I have organised myself well enough to catch Holy Communion there with another British expat who comes and goes in our town - one of the very few. He is himself a Methodist and has lived in this country for most of the last 13 years. He is called TJ and has a high profile with some of my NGO colleagues and with many Africans too. He tells me he has been involved in various development projects - mainly to do with education and training - both here up-country and back in the Kombos. It is good to be able to compare African experiences with someone of a similar age and sector background.

Neither TJ nor I could make much of the service or get a great deal from it devotionally or spiritually. The priest, a Nigerian who delivered the service in English stopping periodically to translate into Mandinka, did lots of dancing and frequently broke into song. When he spoke he sometimes made statements which sounded unusual to a traditional church goer from the UK such as 'Your standard of living depends upon your experience of God!' There was a good deal of drumming and there seemed to be no Lord's Prayer. Neither of us felt the occasion had produced the appropriate state of consciousness to receive the host when the time came - nor did either of us think we would be likely to return for another service subsequently. I note from my guide books that there is an Anglican church at Bansang about 20 kilometres further east along the main South Bank Road [a dirt road though a main road] and I will try that sometime soon.

Practicalities

I bought a beautifully simple and effective palm fan for five dalasi recently. Each such fan is a work of art being made from one unbroken sprig of palm with the leaves plaited into one another and utilising no other materials. They are very commonly used here by the Africans to fan embers into new life as well as to keep cool.

At last my water filter is producing something drinkable. For a long time now the output has been tainted by the new filter candle that I had to install even though I followed the advice given by a number of colleagues and boiled and scrubbed it before installation.

Given the conditions, some things here assume a huge importance compared with back home. For example one's water filter, one's fan, minor health problems which can require medicines or medical attention that aren't readily available here, a patch of shade when one is walking from A to B can make all the difference to the effort output, the scope for taking a nap during the day often essential to recharge one's batteries, one's laptop/netbook computer, one's mobile phone (there are no landlines as an alternative here up-country for most people when one loses one's phone or when there are technical issues with it), one's mosquito net, a torch after dark (solar, wind-up or battery operated ... the full range is used), a short wave radio, cold water, fly screens on doors and windows, fly spray and the state of repair of one's sandals. All these things can be the difference between a life that is bearable or not.

A Naming Ceremony for our *Kunda*

Faa Bakari, our compound head, has just told me that the high point of this Wednesday's naming ceremony for baby Sariang should be between 10 and 11am in the morning and I will be contacted to be notified that proceedings have begun. I was hoping to be able to join in the celebrations after work at 4pm but will now have to sound out how my absence during working hours will be received. Not only that but I am being given another set of African clothes and this time a hat too. These clothes are grander than previously, consisting of a three piece white ensemble called a *nyeti abdu*. It consists of pantaloons, a long collarless shirt that reaches down to my shins and a much thicker white over garment. This latter has sleeves like a wizard's which splay out at their wrist ends. These ends are then normally worn by being folded back up the arm so that ultimately they reach and rest on my shoulders. I get the impression that I am regarded as a key figure in the proceedings as baby Sariang is my namesake. I hope I don't have to sacrifice a chicken or even worse a sheep because, if I have understood what I was told correctly, a sacrifice is involved at some stage. The ceremony I am told formally confirms the baby's name and marks the first time that mother and baby may leave the compound, it being 8 days after the birth.

Baby Sariang's Naming Ceremony: As forewarned I was called at short notice from the education office to attend the formal part of the ceremony - remarkably only a couple of hours later than predicted. I was given pride of place in a seat at the front of the gathering flanked by village elders. The ceremony was conducted in Mandinka with Islamic prayers uttered periodically. I asked Faa Bakari whether I was expected to make a speech to which he replied 'You can make a speech if you want.' This left me wondering whether I was

Faa Bakari, my compound head, Mohamed, his son-in-law and baby Sariang at his naming ceremony

Fatou Marong – mother of baby Sariang at his naming ceremony

'Faa Bakari's senior wife, Ndella, in the centre, with Jainaba, her daughter, to the right and Sibo at the front

supposed to or not. However I decided that to do so was best, so as to demonstrate my regard for the significance of the ceremony and as a vehicle to be able express the honour and gratitude I felt about the baby being named after me. This latter point formed the main thrust of my brief oration along with a request for Allah to grant Baby Sariang a long, happy and successful life. I hoped the implied assumption that baby Sariang's life was not already writ did not contravene any deeply held Islamic beliefs which I vaguely recall from my brief earlier learning on Islam it probably did. I had to stop speaking periodically for the interpreter next to me to pass on my words to the assembled guests in their tribal language. There must have been about seventy or eighty present with the women sitting opposite the men in a less organised fashion. At one point I was presented with some kola nuts to eat. They struck me as almost inedibly bitter even though they have a special meaning here and are used for special occasions only. The accompanying rice paste which had been pounded together with sugar and milk was a thankful relief to my palate.

This formal part of the ceremony concluded, I returned to work assuming that the proceedings would be complete soon after I left. However when I arrived back at the compound after work several hours later celebrations were still underway and the compound yard was full of the sound of the women folk chanting and drumming. There was a real drive to the rhythm and a great deal of repetition in a manner that one feels can't have changed for centuries. All manner of objects were improvised as drums including my jerry cans, various cooking vessels and much more with whistles and clapping in accompaniment. All this was undertaken by the women only, some of whom broke spontaneously into the most energetic solo dances involving unbelievably rapid hip gyrations. Given the sheer bulk of most of the main dancers one wondered how they were able to sustain the pace and the duration of the dances they gave us. The sound of traditional African chanting and singing, often unaccompanied, which I have already experienced here on several occasions, is always haunting, moving and exquisite especially when performed by the women or the children.

Eventually this traditional musical element became swamped by some unbelievably loud amplified, electronic music which was nevertheless unmistakably African in origin. It was provided by a strange looking, itinerant DJ with his equipment who had been engaged for these celebrations which were scheduled to carry us through the evening after the formal event. This individual accompanied most of what he played with his own solo dancing which was even more energetic, feverish and intense than that produced by the women earlier.

Francis Moore says that:

... They [the natives] are very naturally jocose and merry and will dance to a drum or a balafeu *[balafon] sometimes four and twenty hours together, dancing now and then very regular and at other times in very odd gestures striving always to outdo one another in nimbleness and activity ...*

A colleague named Lamin returned to the education offices today after a trip back to the Kombos where he had been to attend the naming ceremony of a relative or friend - I was not sure which. He related a very sad story about the mother of the new baby being named. Though she left the clinic after the birth she had to return to it as she developed breathing difficulties and other problems. Tragically she died on the day of the naming ceremony itself. One wondered what circumstances conspired for things to turn out so badly. Lamin didn't seem to know precise details. The maternal mortality rate here is more than 50 times greater than back home in the UK.

Husbandry, Landscape and Climate

Today I noticed that our neighbours in the next compound keep what look like Guinea Fowl. In fact I am told they are **Guinea Fowl**. Apparently it is not uncommon here to go out into the bush and collect the eggs of wild specimens and then establish a small domesticated brood back home in one's compound by getting chickens to hatch the first batch so as to provide a further source of eggs and meat.

Moore records:

> ... *The poultry puts me in mind of Guinea Fowls that are of a dark colour with white spots and blue and red about the heads ... these are generally esteemed to be the tame fowl of Africa but that is a mistake, they are wild as pheasants in England ...*

I personally came across one compound where the flock of Guinea Fowl being reared were pure white.

Have I ever made mention of **the termite mounds** here? They are to be seen frequently when travelling through the bush – one comes across a cluster of them usually – with mounds set a few feet or sometimes several yards apart. They have strange and irregular shapes which look gives the impression of a lunar landscape. One half of me expects the Clangers to suddenly appear out of a burrow.

In terms of the landscape generally I have yet to see it in the dry season. Currently everywhere is very lush but I am told that it is quite different during the dry season and I look forward to seeing it then. I shouldn't have to wait long as the rain now seems to be tailing off.

There is a particular symmetry about today's date as its 10.10.10. I checked the time at 3.10am this morning having gradually surfaced from sleep due to the heat build-up following the scheduled loss of power and hence my fan between 2 and 2.30am. I woke slowly through that period of consciousness when we re-run our experiences in an altered form and succession – they ebb and flow and speak to us and somehow, for me, usually grant respite and peace through some kind of resolution. I have sometimes wondered whether this state will be part of the transitional experience that is awaiting us all when we leave this place – when the familiar canons of time and space cease to apply and we proceed to the next stage.

The sun is very hot today and everyone is staying deep within the umbrae of whatever pools of shade they can find. When the Africans move, they move slowly from one patch of shade to the next – they know from long experience and perhaps an inborn sense that this is wise. For **the man who runs the tyre repair shop** on the main street of our town, whose services I seem to need all too frequently for my motorbike, this dodging of the blinding sun and burning heat is part of a daily routine. Around midday he will leave the flimsy corrugated awning that sticks out from the front of his small workshop. It is supported by two slender poles on its fore-edge. Under it he spends the morning hours but by midday it becomes too much of a heat-trap to be bearable and he crosses the road to take up a new position opposite sitting and leaning against a convenient stretch of wall until his next customer appears. The narrow strip of shade the wall offers at this time is just wide enough to protect him from direct sunlight. I often wonder if he looks back across the street to his workplace with its various accoutrements and considers his life there with some degree of meditative contemplation and overview.

The girls, always busy, are conserving their strength by sitting around tending to one another's hair. What are called corn rows in London are popular here and the girls seem to be able to plait their hair for one another to a very high standard. In fact generally their hair seems to be beautifully well kept – there is too a real creativity in their approach to styling.

Africans are very generous with their food. Whenever food appears you are invited to share it. People will do this even when they have insufficient for themselves. If an individual is eating for example even a boiled egg, a piece of fruit or a sandwich, they will offer you some. However their diet consists mainly of rice which is eaten two or three times a day and constitutes the overwhelming proportion of almost any meal. At breakfast rice will often be pounded with groundnuts and then cooked with milk powder [if they have any – it's expensive] or just water and eaten as rice porridge. For lunch, sometimes with a small amount of meat or fish and with a few vegetables if the budget stretches to it, rice will be eaten with a sauce. Left-overs will serve as dinner.

Benechin, a Senegalese rice dish, in preparation

Moore:

... rice which is ... esteemed their choicest food...

After copious hand washing, food is eaten normally from a large communal food bowl with one's right hand. Allowances are made for *toubabs* who don't have the dexterity and they may use a spoon. If one uses a spoon then one may use one's left hand – though this will often be remarked upon. One participant will usually take it upon themselves, as the need arises, to break up the small amount of meat or fish, if there is any, with their right hand and share it around the bowl putting a piece in front of each participant; similarly with the vegetables. To do this with one hand can take great skill especially when anything is tough. Further and not uncommonly, the women will sit at one food bowl and the men at another though this practice is not rigidly adhered to in my experience. The food can be very hot - scotch bonnet chilli peppers are frequently used. Particularly popular dishes are *Domoda* made with a groundnut sauce, *Yasser* with onions and a mustard sauce, *Mbahal* [Wolof] or *Nyankatang* [Mandinka] a dry dish with crumbled dried fish, locust beans and steamed rice all mixed together and *Benechin*, a Senegalese rice dish fried in palm oil. Jumbo, a common brand of seasoning cube, is frequently used both in cooking dishes and to sprinkle over food when eaten.

A Trip to Bansang: Echoes of the Past

I took a trip to Bansang, a town and landing place further upriver, to find an appropriate church. On my way I was excited to see my first **troop of baboons** - about thirty or forty of them of all ages and sizes. They were crossing the South Bank Road just outside Janjanbureh - quite a spectacle. I have heard conflicting reports of how careful to be with them. A work colleague has told me never to approach them - especially the large males which you should not look at directly as this may be interpreted as a threat. When I asked my compound head about this he told me that this was nonsense and that they would never attack a man. I'm not convinced!

Apparently I have been misled about Bansang churches as there is no Anglican church, only a Catholic one, a Methodist one and an Evangelical one not in the Anglican Communion. I had a warm welcome from the latter and was invited to join the service so I did. Praying consisted of walking around uttering 'Halleluiahs' and making statements about how lucky we are to have Jesus, mighty Jesus etc. No Lord's Prayer, no communion and the only words I recognised were '... through the love of God and the fellowship of the Holy Spirit' at the end. I was asked to introduce myself to the congregation and give a brief account of myself which I did. This seems to be the custom here when participating as a newcomer in any church service.

The road from my island to Bansang follows the course of the river but at a little distance from it. In Francis Moore's time somewhere between this road and the river was a settlement named **Brucoe** which he tells us '... is a large town ... which is inhabited by people of the Mundigo race but strict followers of Mahomet ...' From his map it must have been close to the present day settlement of Kesereh – perhaps Kesereh is Brucoe renamed. At least one present day local inhabitant from across the river told me that they are one and the same. The Royal African Company factory close by also took its name from Brucoe and was at or very near to the river bank itself. Like other factories it was used as a holding place for tradable goods which would eventually be sent downriver to James Island or further upriver to be used in exchange for goods the RAC wished to take back ultimately to Europe or America. Amongst goods in transit downriver might be slaves, gold, ivory and beeswax and much else. During Moore's stay along the Gambia he became the factor [or agent] at Brucoe for a period [as he did at other factories along the river at different times] – his employer feeling that they could trust in his diligence and honesty to run it in an orderly and efficient manner.

Tales from the Regional Education Directorate

We have a number of **secretaries at work**. As far as I can tell they are mostly unpaid and do their jobs to gain work experience - like a so called 'internship' in the UK; the Regional Director's secretary may be an exception to this - I'm not sure. However they have no computers of their own and usually their keyboard skills are very poor or non-existent. They will just as readily turn their hands to cooking the office lunch and spend a lot of time running errands for people. They will attempt to type the occasional letter if they can manage to get time on a computer and do some filing occasionally. I noticed when I went into the office recently that one of them who had **recently** been **married** looked very worried. When I enquired as to the problem she said quite openly that she was worried because her virginity was being checked by her new husband's family later this week as she was about to be 'given' to her husband for the first time. I think it was the process that worried her and not any thought that she might not pass through the check with an adverse report. I was told too that she is about to spend a week and a half with him on what she described as their 'honeymoon' and she has not been alone with him before. When I asked where they were going on their honeymoon she said to his family compound. She looks extremely nervous about the whole business. I have always assumed she's upwards of twenty-five years old but she tells me she is in fact twenty. Forgetting momentarily that I was dealing with a culture entirely different from my own I suggested her new husband was probably just as nervous as she about the whole thing and that she should not worry so much. Then the differences dawned on me and I asked whether he was already married. He was she said and had four children by his first wife. I asked whether his other wife was much older than herself and she said not much. It brought home to me how quickly life unfolds for girls here as they move into womanhood. Further this intern secretary tells me she has been in phone contact with the other wife for her advice about what to do and how to respond to her husband during their first nights together. She says she has no objections to her husband having another wife and he will be able to trust her fidelity with absolute confidence. She also tells me that she misses me when I'm not at work for any reason and that she likes my mobile phone. She has expressed fantasies about coming to England with me at Christmas for she knows I have planned a brief return. She says we will be more than just friends. I have had some difficulty in reconciling all these statements with one another!

Moore:

> *When a man takes home his wife he makes a feast at his house to which everybody that is willing comes without the form of an invitation for they don't use much ceremony that way ... The woman is brought upon men's shoulders to her husband's house ... with a veil over her face which she keeps on till such time she has been in bed with her husband ... if he should declare to the people that his wife was not a maid when he took her home it would be looked upon as a very great scandal to him ...*

I went out **'on trek'** with colleagues yesterday for the first time. We visited some of our directorate schools. I was shocked by the poor level of resourcing which has to be seen to be believed. They often have very few and sometimes no books, little in the way of educational equipment, sometimes fewer teachers than they need and usually no electricity. I quickly realised that my idea of finding someone in the UK to donate a few old computers is inappropriate for all except our directorate office. This power issue also means they have no copying facilities so they can't even copy essential pro-formas, circulars etc. Wall displays, where they exist, are usually drafted by hand.

More sad news - this time from Amat a Senior Education Officer with whom I share an office. His nephew who was named after him and in whom Amat therefore took a special interest has just died - suddenly - he was only nine years old. Apparently his family had sent him north to Dakar to start a new life with his Senegalese relatives there in the big city. He was excited about his future. Within a few days he seems to have caught some bug, Amat didn't know what precisely and to have died quickly within a matter of days. Amat is very upset and left work early so that he could be on hand at home to console his relatives. Before he did so we discussed the mysteries of life and of God's plan; we agreed that in some way Amat's nephew needed to be with God now; that the boy has simply gone onto the next phase as we all will but just sooner than anyone would have expected. I told Amat that I would pray for the boy and the safe passage of his soul which Amat thanked me for and which he seemed to appreciate very much. It is very common here when deaths occur for close relatives not to be able to give you a medical explanation of what has happened and oddly to the Westerner they don't seem to worry that they can't; they do not seem to push the doctors involved for an explanation. It just doesn't seem important to them.

There are a few observations on **my work environment**, the regional education office, that are worth recording. I have already mentioned that 'secretaries' have no computers allocated to them but nor do any of the other staff. There are a few desktops and laptops which get handed around and used by different people at different times as needed. I have always used my own notebook computer. There seems to be no culture established of corresponding by email although occasionally colleagues do – but not all of them even have an email address. In fact computers seem to be used more frequently for leisure purposes than work purposes – during working hours. As I mentioned earlier sitting at a computer is not always viewed as an indicator that someone is engaged on a work related project or task – and colleagues are almost as likely to be accessing Facebook or engaged in another non-work pursuit when they do. Of course this is partly a consequence or availability of a good connection to the internet and intranet. Even at the best of times the connection is painfully slow and one can lose it altogether for days at a time. Sometimes the link for the whole of the country is lost.

Printing paper is another issue. It is scarce and hence is used sparingly. Other stationery items aren't available at all and so are often provided by the employees themselves without rancour or complaint.

Further there are no land-line telephones and no office mobile phones. Again therefore one is thrown back on using one's own for work purposes and what's more one's own precious phone credit.

There is too in terms of work culture no strict delineation between work and non-work time. If suddenly one is needed to work in the evening or even on a Saturday or Sunday or both this is accepted without question by staff at all levels and it doesn't mean that there will necessarily be corresponding time off in lieu. On the other hand one can excuse oneself for a couple of hours in order to go shopping at the local food market during designated working time and no-one objects. All of this seems strange to the average Westerner.

However I have great optimism that my time here will be productive and go well. The new Regional Director seems to have started his new posting well. He gives the impression of being a quiet and considered man.

Bansang Again

Today is Sunday and I have taken **a further trip to Bansang** to try **the Catholic Church** there this time. On the way I saw

Tree with an interesting root formation close to the river crossing landing stage at Bansang

two separate troops of baboons – one on the way and I believe a different one on the way back.

At last I have found a church service here up-country where I felt a spiritual presence! I recognised much of the liturgy which was delivered both in English and local tribal languages. I assume we got the Lord's Prayer but I was unable to identify it for certain. Importantly we maintained silences and solemnity at particular moments which made sense within my own established tradition. I took the Eucharist in one kind and spoke briefly to the assistant priest at the end of the service. I am hoping my Anglican affiliation which I declared to him isn't a problem for them. This priest seemed unsure when I explained my position to him. He will consult the head priest when he can.

Though we are coming out of the wet season now and the humidity levels have dropped they remain significant and increase any tendency one might have to sweat. One consequence of these conditions is that the bank notes are always damp and filthy. If the plague is lurking here somewhere I am sure that the banknotes will become a prime carrier of the disease.

Back at the Compound

We are into the latter part of October now and tonight **Mama [Mariam]**, one of our compound children, has decided to come and sit with me at my kitchen table whilst she does her Maths homework and I work at my small computer typing up my reflections. She is eight years old and seems to enjoy the fact that we are engaged in independent but similar activities at the same time around the same table. This is exactly the kind of satisfaction I detected in my own daughters at her age under similar circumstances. In fact Mama exhibits, perhaps unremarkably, many behavioural and other traits in common with our children in the West even though each day, she is imbibing a matrix of values, beliefs, cultural and religious practices quite different from our own. That there is this common bedrock in human kind surely explains how those from such different cultural contexts can and do relate and co-exist often so frequently, so successfully. I have never been in any doubt that feelings towards me here are positive and supportive even though I am still learning how to behave and sometimes get it wrong.

Francis Moore tells us that along the banks of the Gambia there are many different peoples but:

the most numerous are called the Mundingoes [Mandinka] ... they are generally of a black colour and well set ...' but '... on the north side of the river ... are a people called Jolloiffs ... [who] ... are much blacker and much handsomer ... for they have not the broad noses and thick lips peculiar to the Mundingoes ...

My journal records:

Mama is very dark like some ,but not all, of my *kunda* family. Her skin is the colour of rich, dark chocolate with a deep blueberry luminescence - it is exquisitely smooth and matt. Her fingernails, toenails and the soles of her feet however lighten almost into a shade of pink. Her hair is very neatly arranged in corn rows running backwards except at the front, where it is plaited and runs diagonally forward to her forehead. When I look at myself it seems remarkable that we can look so different and yet share so much in common. When I visit schools here many of the children have never seen a white person before or, if they have, only infrequently. They can be frightened and on one occasion I had to leave a classroom quickly when a very young child, perhaps about three or four years of age, became hysterical at the sight of me. Further I have noticed often that when they inspect me they will check my bare feet in their open sandals just to be sure that the whiteness goes all the way down to my toes.

Moore writes of the natives:

> ... when I went through any of their towns they almost all came to shake hands except some of the women who having never seen any white men ran away from me as fast as they could ...

Although there are a couple of volunteer colleagues billeted here in my town I spend the majority of time at home and therefore within an African ethos. There is a straightforwardness of intent and simplicity of life here that gives clarity and is comforting. Generally there seems to be little sense of irony, and sarcasm is usually entirely misunderstood and can be taken quite literally. Of course protocols can be complex or at least elaborate. For example greetings are highly ritualistic – between Africans they often seem endless. A series of standard salutations, questions and answers are exchanged in a time-honoured sequence. 'Peace be with you', 'Peace returns to you', 'How are you?', 'I am fine. How are you?', 'How are your compound people?', 'They are fine. How are yours?', 'I hope there is no trouble there?' and so on. Participants will then often go on to exchange prayers for one another and one another's family. Again there seems to be a conventional order in which the prayers are uttered becoming more and more fulsome as they succeed one another.

20.10.10. I have just noticed that I have **a gecko** living with me. I think it lives behind the cupboard in my kitchen/living room. Perhaps it will help to keep the insect life in check though I am hoping that it doesn't find a way into my mosquito net whilst I am in there sleeping. When I mentioned the gecko to one of the girls in my compound she said she would get one of the boys to catch and kill it for me. I said no I'd rather keep the gecko thanks. She voiced a belief held commonly here that lizards are poisonous and spread disease. Apparently they are harmless and there is a campaign, no doubt sponsored by one charity or another, to change this thinking. I am told that part of the campaign involves people travelling around giving lecturers on the subject to rural communities in which they put live geckos in their mouths to demonstrate that they have no fear of this and prove that they are harmless.'

Pain Creeps Up!

22.10.10: As I feared might happen **an in-growing toenail** I detected only 6 weeks before leaving the UK, when there seemed insufficient time to take any drastic action to remedy it, is now very painful. Medical advice I took then suggested that with the right self-nursing I could stave off the problem before it became acute but this has not happened. In fact I think it might be infected in spite of my giving it a bathe and an application of antiseptic cream a couple of times a week recently. Having checked further on the internet for info on what to do I have now decided to implement the above treatment using hot water with salt as well as antiseptic cream on a daily basis. I am also taking antibiotics to get rid of any infection I might have. Here it is possible to buy antibiotics without a prescription. I sincerely hope this works because I would not wish to throw myself on the mercy of any of the local clinics which other Westerners tell me are to be strictly avoided. Two of our *kunda* girls, Hawa Jallow and Hawa Bah, took me along to the local pharmacy here to procure the antibiotics. Like most *bitiks* here it was very easy to miss and certainly I had never noticed it before although I must have walked passed it many times. It has no signage and is situated near one of the intersections of a couple of our dirt roads [most of our roads here are laid out in a grid arrangement]. Inside, this inconspicuous establishment consisted of a not very recently whitewashed rectangular room about 12ft by 10ft with three or four shelves across most but not the entire length of the back wall opposite the door. These shelves held a sparse number and variety of plastic jars. There was a counter between me and them which prevented public access into the room for any more than a couple of feet of its depth from the entrance. The pharmacist was an old man untidily dressed with two or three days of stubble on his face. After some discussion about the number of antibiotic capsules I was requesting he wrapped up 30 into a cone shaped twist of old newspaper and told me to take two twice a day for 5 days. This transaction was conducted mainly in Mandinka through my *kunda* girls who were translating for me. I decided not to question the inconsistency between the number of capsules and the dosage instructions especially since I know from experience that people here are commonly and notoriously deficient in being able to perform even the most basic mental arithmetic and thought that it would do me no harm to extend this prescribed course of antibiotics. Whenever we go to the local bar here in our town the barman relies always on our figures when it comes to calculating the final bill. He relies ultimately upon his instinct regards whether we can be trusted or not rather than on his own arithmetical skills.

More on Work

We had a useful meeting at work today as preparation for a larger meeting tomorrow which is Saturday. It consisted of all key Directorate staff and head teachers within the region. On Monday we lose the Regional Director again [he only returned late yesterday] as he has to go to Basse for a CCM [Co-ordinating Committee Meeting – Gambian equivalent of an Ofsted inspection of a region's educational provision]. This is typical of his desultory presence to date.

Regional inspections here are worthy of further comment. The Co-ordinating Committee Meeting is the focus with reports on school and directorate visits and assessments which are channelled back to it. A CCM consists of up to approximately a hundred people sitting as a group meeting including all regional directors, various senior Ministry of Education staff and key managers from the regional directorate under scrutiny. It is chaired by the Permanent Secretary for Education and co-chaired by the Minister of Education. They are reminiscent of a parliamentary select committee in set up and tone. Proceedings can be bizarre. On one occasion I sat through a 30 minute report on the impact of a project to distribute 'free sanitary pads' to girl students in upper basic schools. The report was delivered by a rather crusty old male senior civil servant from the Ministry. The co-chair, the female Minister of Education, was clearly in two minds about whether this item should be in process in the way it was, frequently commenting that these matters are very private matters in our culture. The committee, which was overwhelmingly male, contributed all sorts of searching questions and comments as well as detailed anecdotes about how the project had been implemented in their own area. e.g. we heard of one school where only well behaved girls were given the items in question, another where male teaching staff had been put in charge of distribution. A young female volunteer colleague sitting next to me, who frequently checked my own responses to all of this by reading my face, threw me knowing glances during the proceedings and looked on with a mixture of incredulity, amusement, occasional horror and not a little embarrassment.

Janjanbureh Prison: I pass this every day on my way to and from work. The prisoners can be identified by their pale blue clothes trimmed with white. They appear to be treated very casually by their guards ... in fact everyone seems to be very relaxed around them. Although all the prisoners that I have seen are male some of the prison guards are female and a good deal smaller than their charges. One I saw had her child with her whilst at work. Sometimes the prisoners sit outside and opposite the prison gates on the other side of the dirt road with either no guard or just one. The way everyone behaves it's as if the prison is an open prison but I don't think it is officially. I think it's just part of the relaxed approach to many things here generally. The chief officer whose exact title escapes me came to the Education Office the other day to see if we could lend him some paper - which we couldn't. Such basic resources are in very short supply here and we don't have enough copier paper sometimes for example to carry out quite important document circulation to schools. Copier and other paper is a rationed commodity here.

Although the prison seems very relaxed I have been warned by a number of people never to photograph it for fear of being caught and having my camera confiscated and perhaps worse. Someone in my compound has also told me that once a prisoner escaped but was soon re-captured and was almost beaten to death in the process. I cannot confirm the truth of this story though if true it might explain the apparently docile nature of the inmates.

The Religious Pulse and an Underlying Animism and Belief in Magic

The rhythm of life here is punctuated by **the call to prayer**. It is broadcast with varying intensities and sometimes falteringly over the township's main mosque's PA system. The call, especially in the evening, will often be embellished by other recitations from the Koran and perhaps elsewhere [for I know not with any certainty] which can go on sometimes interminably ... it is as if life's experience cannot be whole or complete without this accompaniment as the day comes to a balmy close.

On Fridays most men will wear their best clothes in the Arab style, many with pill box caps. On any occasion when the call occurs an interlocutor is likely to excuse themselves from your company precipitously to go and pray at the scheduled time. They will recite their prayers audibly to themselves and fellow prayers and appear not to be disturbed by those nearby within earshot who might continue to converse or generate noise completely unrelated to their intercessional activities.

There appears to be no obvious religious friction in The Gambia as far as I can see and Islam here appears not to have that intolerant or hard edge that is sometimes associated with it. It is deeply rooted in the people but is permeated by an underlying animism as is Christianity here. There is something to be admired in the way Islam, Christianity and the colonial legacy generally have failed to eradicate completely an underlying distinctly African nature and tradition.

Sources can vary slightly but in The Gambia at the time of writing approximately 90 per cent of the people are Muslim, 8 per cent Christian, less than 2 per cent adhere to traditional religions and there are a few Hindus. There are very few atheists amongst the indigenous population.

Commonly religious forms are syncretised with African Traditional Religions.

On my way from work today I walked past a group of women from the town on Jackson Street - the street on which I live. They were walking in the opposite direction and were dressed in their best clothes even though today is not Friday. I learnt later from Jainaba, a fellow compound family member that they were likely to have been on their way to pay their last respects to a lady in the town who has just died. It is the tradition here to call on the bereaved family as well turned out as one can and to gift money to help with the loss ... often even before the burial which occurs, in accordance with Islamic law, as quickly as possible after the death has occurred.

I was told too that another death has occurred very recently in the town. It was a man in his thirties who works at the IEC (Independent Electoral Commission). Fatou thinks the cause is malaria but as usual no one seems sure. Life expectancy here is so much lower than back home ... it's around 60 years for both men and women.

A Strange Day at Janjanbureh Upper Basic School: 'Falling Down'

My journal records:

I was working in my office today, which is situated on the Directorate campus just across the dirt road from the above school, when I heard a commotion from the school. Intense screams and shrieks and high pitched noises of a disturbance emanated from the school. Then I began to see girls, one by one, perhaps at approximately 10 second intervals, run from one of the classroom blocks in a highly hysterical state. Each was chased by a group of boys and once caught each was then pinned to the ground. The school compound began to fill up with many such pursuits and captures and eventually, I counted no less than eight groupings each consisting of a single girl pinned to the ground by a group of boys at various points across the school yard. The girls were in a highly hysterical state, rolling around and kicking, shrieking, flailing their arms, trying to escape the boys who were restraining them. A senior colleague in my own office told me that this was a recurring problem and that it afflicted particularly this school across the road and another elsewhere within our Central River Region. A third school at Basse [Basse Santa Su] further east in the Upper River Region is said to have the same problem. The girls, I was told, were being restrained for their own good. They had seen the devil. It was a problem that was long standing. It affected the girls only and usually the older ones. No one knew what was to be done about it.

Eventually one of our Directorate pick-up trucks went to the assistance of the school and in batches ferried the still struggling girls, who were unceremoniously loaded into the back of the truck with some boys piled on top of them to keep them there, to the local hospital or to their homes depending on the severity of the hysteria.

My African colleague, a graduate and relatively well educated man, explained that sometimes this just happens and that some locations, like this school, are particularly bad for the presence of the Devil. There was nothing to be done about it ... except to move the school and he believed ultimately everyone would come around to this view. I explained that the average Western mind would have difficulty in accepting this and in leaving the issue intellectually unchallenged in this way. He felt that it was foolish not to see that there are many things which we simply cannot understand or control. I wanted to go on to say to him that of course that must be true but that to call it possession by the Devil was to give an explanation which as far as I could see was insufficiently grounded in evidence. But I could see that as far as he was concerned no further discussion was necessary and that this would cut no ice with him at all ... I knew that I would be introducing empirical criteria that he did not need or accept - they would be entirely foreign to him and inconsistent with the cultural matrix of beliefs and knowledge through which he perceived the world and coped with it.

During my time with the Directorate the above happened regularly at the school and we went through periods when it happened almost every week; sometimes even several times a week. I discovered too that it had been happening for many years. No African I spoke to doubted the authenticity of these cases including the Regional Director. They were believed to be cases of devil possession though they were referred to usually as cases of 'falling down'. In fact this was the term in widespread use in The Gambia for this phenomenon which occurred more generally than simply in specific schools or other locations. We subsequently had a case in my own compound. The victim was a quite large young lady from a neighbouring compound. She grew so violent during the attack that two of her own quite well built brothers were unable to pin her down and the furniture in the room where this happened went flying; somehow even a quite heavy double bed was turned completely upside-down. I was close by when this took place, just outside my own little room/house just two rooms further along the veranda. As the commotion continued suddenly everyone, including my landlord and compound leader Faa Bakari, exited the room as quickly as they could and left the victim alone inside. They looked terrified and running swiftly they retreated to a safe distance across the other side of our compound shouting to me that I should follow suit. Perhaps foolishly, as a non-believer in the Devil and resisting quite deliberately their way of seeing this occurrence, I decided to stand my ground. I leant as casually as I could against the veranda balustrade just 10 or 12 feet from the entrance to the room in question and waited for her to emerge which she did within a few minutes. I think I must have felt that their belief in devil possession somehow made them more vulnerable than I and at the same time I wanted them to witness a different response to events. When she emerged from the room she looked otherworldly; more animal than human. Her pupils appeared to be dilated and she scanned everything as if a predator searching for its prey. My fellow compound people continued to beg me to run. I tried to look unmoved and relaxed but braced myself ready to defend myself. She was a big woman with strength and youth on her side and I knew I would have to treat her roughly to have any hope of avoiding serious injury to either of us should she attack me. In the event, though she fixed me with her eyes, to which I stared back defiantly, nothing happened before her condition subsided and she ultimately collapsed into a state of exhaustion though it was some time before anyone would approach her to render assistance.

A Medical Deterioration

At this point in my stay it became clear that my **in-growing toe nail** was not getting any better. In spite of my best efforts the condition was now becoming quite advanced and very painful. I was limping badly. I knew my foot was infected but it was not responding to the earlier mentioned regime of hot salt baths, antiseptic cream and anti-biotics. On everyone's advice, including my own, I decided to travel back to the coast to get treatment at the clinic recommended by my NGO with which they had a contract for the medical support of all staff. This seemed especially necessary as facilities and standards of care and hygiene at our local clinic up-country were reportedly very basic. Indeed I remembered being told by our doctor on the coast before I left for my up-country posting that In relation to my intended location I must never let anyone stick a needle into me without them phoning him first.

Francis Moore:

> *18th September 1734 ... Mr Phillips having almost cured his leg went to Fatatenda over land, in a canoe, the road hence being now some feet underwater ... 26th ... came down Mr Phillips with his leg in a most miserable condition he having struck it against the stump of a tree ... it was so bad that without relief he must inevitably lose his life ... he therefore designed to make the best of his way down to James Fort*

and the next morning I hired some people to row him down to Brucoe.

On the 2nd October the people which carried Mr Phillips returned with the melancholy account of his dying about 12 miles from Brucoe; that they carried him there and that Mr Railton, the Company's Chief there, had buried him.

My own return to the coast was delayed by 5 or 6 days as I was told daily that one of our regional office vehicles was about to make the trip. Given the increasing difficulty I had in walking I was reluctant to use public transport ... a gruelling experience even in full health. In the event the office vehicle suffered one delay after another and eventually I got a lift with one of our own NGO vehicles which had travelled up-country to bring an independent monitor who was undertaking a survey of our work for our organisation. By the time I got back to the coast the pain was severe and walking had become hopping.

Return to the Coast

My journal continues:

I am down in the Kombos to seek help with my in-growing toenail. My organisation has referred me to something called Africmed. I have booked myself into Mama's Hotel in Fajara, some twenty minutes' walk from our in-country HQ, whilst I undergo treatment. However a friend of the hotel's landlady who kindly offered to give me a lift to Africmed turns out to be **a Dutch nurse** who has lived here for some time. She says she is familiar with such medical problems, is in the process of obtaining a nursing practice licence for The Gambia. She offered to examine my foot before I see Africmed, an organisation which she does not particularly recommend. One's confidence is easily disturbed about the medical provision here on the basis of what one has seen and learned already and I agreed to this. Not only did she examine my foot but gave it a bath in washing powder, removed some of the nail and dressed the toe after applying some antiseptic cream to dispel the infection. She thought antibiotics could be and were best avoided but that we wouldn't know this until I had her treatment daily for at least two weeks. She has counselled strongly against my agreeing to any surgery in The Gambia given the quality of the treatment available.

Mama's Hotel, Restaurant and Bar is situated up a dirt road near the Timbooktu Bookshop [a most unexpected and very great blessing being well stocked with a good range of recent literary fiction and non-fiction as well as classic titles] in Fajara on the Bakau Road and is next to the southern perimeter of the MRC. Sometimes I am told monkeys can be seen from Mama's outdoor bar/restaurant area – where one spends all ones time at the hotel when not in one's room. The monkeys live in the extensive MRC grounds but so far they have eluded me.

It is 2nd November and my toe continues to be very painful. Josie, the Dutch nurse, has dressed it for me with the usual treatment but my hotel and other expenses here are mounting and my NGO won't pay these for me unless I see Africmed to confirm my condition. Hence I must go to them in spite of Josie's advice.

Africmed recommend toenail removal after the infection has settled down which will only be achieved they think through antibiotics. I agree to their taking over my medical management and the daily dressing of my foot at the clinic but seeing conditions there I also insist that I will only be prepared to undergo toenail removal back in the UK. My NGO HQ in London is working on the whole issue for me and will get back to me as soon as they can about what expenses they will or will not be prepared to take on to remedy the situation.'

Killing Time

Friday 5th November. I have now been in Fajara since last Saturday when I arrived here from up-country. It is a strange period because I have been hoping each day that my NGO will clarify what support they can offer in my situation. I continue to await news as to whether they will fly me back to the UK for treatment. My daily dressings continue at Africmed. As I write I await news on whether one of our NGO vehicles can take me to this clinic and return me to my hotel today or not. In lieu of this they will pay for a taxi to do so.

I have spent the days reading, moving between V.S. Naipaul whose fearless, uncompromising honesty and integrity I find so compelling and T.S. Eliot and have otherwise done some writing, sitting, eating, drinking and talking, sometimes to Josie, the Dutch nurse. Josie has very strong opinions about things especially The Gambia and Gambians and they are not very complimentary. She can be very aggressive and negative about them like some other ex-pat Europeans I've met here. Many congregate at Mamas. There is one, **a Brit, who is 79 years old who continually gives of his 'wisdom'** to all and sundry making statements in a very loud and clear voice about his views and colourful life. His output can be self-revealing, abusive, offensive and often just incoherent and is usually peppered with expletives but can be entertaining. If you happen to wind up as his interlocutor on occasion as I have this can be seriously embarrassing. Statements broadcast that I noted from just one session were as follows:

'... the thing about The Gambia is that you pay f*** all and you get f*** all. I've just bought a Chinese electric razor for 450 dalasi [about £10.00] and I hope the f***ing thing works'

'... the trouble is that the f***ing Chinese have bought up Africa from the corrupt f***ing Africans who run it.'

'I've just received my latest bank statement from the UK. I thought my step-son had stolen another f***ing £30,000 but apparently he hasn't this time.'

'I once had a villa in Spain which I sold there – about ten years ago. Apparently the Spanish are now after me about it all around the UK because according to their records my ex-wife and not I owned it so that I had no right to sell it. The Spanish are just like the Gambians... their records are f***ed'

'What you need to understand about Africans is that they are all prostitutes basically!'

'... You get to my age and you've had enough sex. I hate these Gambian prostitutes; they've got so little in their heads they're not even interesting to talk to. I've got one coming to see me later tonight and I'm going to give her £15 just to f... off.'

'The problem here is with the NGOs – typical f...ing do-gooders. They have helped to keep too many Africans alive – that's why there are these resource issues – too many f...ing people.'

Of course this man is not taken seriously by most, being written off as the worst kind of anachronistic, insensitive, colonial stereotype, but he remains a very poor advert for the Brits here in particular and for Europeans more generally and he is not alone amongst them in making outrageous and offensive anti-African statements but he is the worse example I've come across. I have made clear to the African bar staff at the hotel, who like many of the Africans I have met here have a very limited capacity for irony or non-literal comprehension of discourse, that his views are an embarrassment to me and that I don't believe they represent a general view on the part of European ex-pats. I said I hoped they didn't think we were all the same as him. I felt it was important to do this – important to try to restore any confidence that they might have had in their white fellow human beings. They said that they are sometimes much offended by some of what they overhear but feel they cannot speak out as this will put their jobs here at risk and employment is very hard to come by.

I continue to kill time and life is punctuated by my daily trips to the clinic for my toe-leaning and dressing. I am conveyed thus either by taxi or an NGO vehicle which takes me there via the Bertil Harding Highway and its continuation the Senegambia Highway which tracks, but stands back a short distance from, the coast.

The building development strung out along this route fights with the bush for supremacy. This road has long stretches of palms of all varieties with fans and sprays of sage green hues thrusting themselves out of the dry red earth. The sparse building stock however continually grows in density - the showy houses are mainly brown or ochre or some other sandy shade. They sport ironwork grills over windows and doorways and often have shoddily produced balustrades on flat rooftops as well as along verandas. Though relatively urban and populated this stretch of road, lying close to and linking the most popular tourist beaches, nevertheless feels hostile to human life as if any incursion made by man is unwelcome, unnatural, incongruous and will be short-lived. Additionally this route boasts a market garden and an area grazed by pigs - the latter presumably being fattened for tourist consumption in this largely Muslim country.

Saturday 06.11.10 ... At last **my temporary return to the UK for medical treatment has been agreed** and booked. I fly this Tuesday changing at Dakar and Brussels and then on to Heathrow. There was a delay in my picking up the ticket from the Brussels's Airlines office earlier today as first I had to travel into Banjul to pick up the cash for it from my NGOs bank as the Fajara branch didn't have £800 in sterling. This was surprising. Picking up the ticket was further complicated by the fact that the President had declared today **a cleaning day** ... one of the more bazaar institutions to be found here ... and then changed his mind. Cleaning days [which can be cancelled or confirmed at the last minute - somehow the final decision gets around amongst the population] are when everything but essential services must stop ... certainly travel is banned. Why - so that all citizens can clean up their compounds, the roads and any public areas generally. If you try to travel on such days you are likely to be stopped and questioned not only at check points but anywhere if the police suspect you are on the move without a sufficiently good reason. I have no idea whether anyone has ever costed this exercise in terms of the economy. I wonder whether the President is a closet Green or perhaps he just likes to exercise his absolute power!

I have been in contact with my *kunda* head, Faa Bakari and have agreed to pay a retainer on my house of 500 dalasi whilst I'm away - in addition he will continue to receive rent money from my employer. I asked Faa Bakari if he was content with this and he said 'You are the head of the family - if that's the arrangement then I accept it as right'. It seems to me that Gambians have a different way from us with these things. People here contribute to their family compounds when they can but continue receiving the benefits of the compound like food and shelter when they cannot. I am told that people here don't starve even though so many are in poverty as internationally defined. I knew that death through starvation was still sometimes a problem in India when I visited in 2005 [this was confirmed by news reports] even though the average income there is much higher than here in The Gambia. I cannot say what effect if any the *kunda* system of care for all its inmates has on an individual's work ethic. I do know that employment here is generally difficult to come by.

Recent reports indicate that **undernourishment in The Gambia** has been increasing and that in the area in which I held my placement, the Central River Region, malnutrition stands at a level which is one of the worst in the country. There have been adverse farming conditions in recent years with the dry season becoming hotter and dryer so that the limits of the Sahel, the sub-Saharan border region, have been creeping further south into the Senegambian savanna.

Even volunteers, especially those serving up-country, with a regular income will often feel they have insufficient food. During my stay I lost a significant amount of weight within just the first few months of my arrival as did most of my colleagues.

But The Gambia is blessed by gluts at certain times of the year of some agricultural products. Oranges [which are usually green in colour and very tart] appear around February/March, mangoes from April/May when they can be found everywhere and of course groundnuts, by far The Gambia's biggest crop, which are harvested in September/October. The nuts are sold mainly to a national marketing board but are always on sale from women and girl street vendors in small bags for a few dalasi. They will usually be roasted in sand or boiled. For me these food items felt like a life saver and a very pleasant one.

I learnt from one of the UK ex-pats I spoke to today that if you have a bank account in the UK and a UK correspondence address you can receive your state pension here drawn through a Gambian bank. This allows ex-pats of pensionable age the ability to live here at an above average level of income. It also means that they receive a winter fuel allowance whilst baking in typically more than 30 degrees of heat.

09.11.10: I am leaving Mama's today after approximately a week and a half of hobbling about here. In some ways I have rather enjoyed the experience with Mama's steady German Swiss tones – somewhat humourless but offering consistency and authority when necessary [elements generally in short supply here] and there's always cheese for breakfast amongst other things in the North European manner – a commodity I welcome so much having had no access to it up-country or anywhere else since I arrived. I've enjoyed so much the leisurely breakfasts alone with only my book, my netbook computer and my notebook to keep me company.

I see Mama on Fridays making short work of the fishmonger when he comes offering his fish in a great mound in his wheel barrow. She chooses only the freshest and seems to dictate the price – he withers before her unfriendly and firm responses. Mama doesn't like the British ex-pat with the loud voice and offensive remarks. He's a resident guest here. I don't think it's the insults to Africans so much that she doesn't like as the very sexy hot-panted young African girl who comes to see him quite regularly. I think it disgusts her and she thinks it lowers the tone of the establishment. Mama gave him notice to quit yesterday on the slightest pretext.

In his journal Francis Moore writes:

... the girls would have people think they are very modest, especially when they are in company, but take them by themselves and they are very obliging for if you would give them a little coral or a silk handkerchief you may take what liberty you please with them.

The present day tourist sex industry on the coast, though it couldn't be more at odds with the strict, traditional, Islamic values operating generally in the country, is conducted quite openly. Scantily clad young women often in very tight clothes with an unmistakable purpose will be abroad at night on the streets, in the restaurants and hotels particularly in the area around the Senegambia Road. Perhaps even more abundant are the young African men who will offer their escort services to the many mainly North European women in their late 40s, 50s and 60s who have come here for their attentions.

These trades allow poverty, loneliness and desire to collide and honesty and innocence, if there be any on either side, are forever lost.

I have also enjoyed filling in the time by means of a text dialogue with a friend in London, namely Ken Hyam, who is a poet and former work colleague. You have no idea how much an exchange with someone on such a topic as the true import of 'Prufrock' and the birth of Modernism makes one feel alive and brings everything into its right perspective whilst sitting in these intense tropical conditions.

One further great bonus has been that at this hotel one can purchase the local lager ice cold and on-tap. Its temperature particularly presents a great temptation in this wearing heat though one tries one's hardest to delay consuming the first glass until a respectable hour in the late afternoon.

There has been some serious reflection on work issues and some related calls to colleagues but this has been piecemeal and with no real engagement from the Regional Director due in part to his frequent absences has little result. However what with casual meetings and sometimes dinner with one's fellow volunteers, dialogues with Ken in the late afternoon and early evening, the opportunity to immerse oneself in a good book and to write one's journal and the ice cold draft lager, this has been a wonderful interlude except for the ever present throbbing and sometimes shooting pain in my toe.

One can never have everything!

Out of Africa

My treatment back in London proved to be problematic and painful. The infection, probably due to my treatment delays up-country followed by the Dutch nurse's brief and all too gentle approach back on the coast, had become so firmly embedded that the antibiotics I was given in Africa failed to have any impact. Two further courses proved to be necessary back in the UK to defeat it. It was as if Africa had quite literally lodged itself deeply within me and was not prepared to give up its claim. In a metaphorical sense this is a feeling that I carry with me to this day.

The removal of the nail had to proceed whilst the infection still raged as the nail was thought to be aiding resistance to its treatment. Avoiding some tempting sacrilegious expressions and choice expletives I will simply report that in pain terms the removal procedure was at the high end of the scale. By Christmas however I was almost ceasing to hobble and at my request VSO did its best to get me back to my placement as soon as possible.

In the time I had left before my flight departure I did some shopping buying a few small gifts for my *kunda* folk – those people who had taken me in in that unfamiliar world I had gone to 3000 miles away. Just little things that you couldn't buy up-country easily but which could be accommodated in my luggage – some lipstick, nail varnish and a few other small cosmetic items in a make-up bag for each of our women and girls; a penknife for fifteen year old Mohamed who did odd jobs for me and lived in the small terraced house next to mine in our compound – that is when he wasn't being turned out for visitors. Finally a Swiss army knife for Faa Bakari and one for his son-in-law, another Mohamed, the police inspector. I took toothpaste and toothbrushes to hand out too though I knew that as soon as the toothpaste ran out the recipients would not meet the expense of buying more locally and would revert to their chewing sticks to keep their teeth clean – the sticks made from the twigs of the jambakatang tree – the tree they used for other purposes too including the making of green tea. I wandered around Brent Cross Shopping Centre on this errand in desultory fashion putting these gifts together with the underlying feeling that in some way for me Africa had changed everything and changed it forever.

Return to Africa

6th January 2011 - And so, early in this New Year, I have been able to re-join a life that has given me so much to think about. It is hard to say precisely what reorganisation takes place within the human psyche, when we know we are leaving a familiar country and its culture of which we are so much a product, to continue a life in another so different. Somehow the journey itself has become otherworldly and symbolic of that psychic transition, of the great distance that must be travelled in every sense between these two worlds. First there has been a five and a half hour delay at the Brussels transfer. This has affected The Gambia-bound passengers only and we are told that this is because the Senegalese authorities, in the wake of friction between Senegal and The Gambia, have decided at short notice that no passengers bound for Banjul will be permitted to touch down at Dakar. This seems churlish considering such passengers normally remain on the aircraft anyway. The airline therefore has had to arrange a separate and direct flight for us to Banjul. The considerable delay has meant that much of my flight from Brussels to my West African destination has taken place during the night-time hours. I was unsure where we were as night fell because the flight tracking screen on the back of the passenger seat in front of me had ceased to function - maybe North Africa or perhaps the Spanish mainland still. Wherever we were the towns we flew over in the intense darkness presented themselves as spectacular webs of luminosity, traceries of the richest brocade with arterial routes of even brighter light running through them and all with an irregular sprinkling of points of light of varying sizes in some cases even more intense. These areas of habitation would then peter-out with just a few fine threads of light running deep into their hinterlands of the densest black until even they became extinguished. This was my pathway, my link back to my home in the African interior – back to the Source – with all the strangeness it held for me.

I am now back at my *kunda* and the girls here have already come to sit with me in the evening to talk. They tell me that though they didn't like to tell me when I first arrived, as they thought it would frighten me, a snake was found in our terrace roof space shortly before I came to live here which they killed. They think it had been eating some of the big rats that lived in the woodshed a short distance across the compound yard from my house. They assured me that both snake and rats were now gone. Nevertheless I found this news somewhat disconcerting.

January 11th. It is now just a few days since my return and the weather has been very acceptable. It is hot during the day but not unduly, reaching the low thirties typically but the evenings are cooler and more importantly there are hardly any insects ... thank God!

Some Cultural Observations

Circumcision: January 12th ... and the girls in my *kunda* have asked me whether I heard the procession passing and I asked them what procession. They said the procession of the boys and girls to be circumcised. I told them I had not and asked what they thought about this and did they know that female circumcision was very controversial. They said they did know this but thought nothing about it really ... it's our tradition they said. They told me that the boys may be circumcised in a clinic or hospital or in the bush but not the girls. I understood them to say that this usually happens between two and six years old but I am not sure. I couldn't help but flinch at the news that the little four year old girl whose mother drops her off each day for us to look after when on her way to work at the women's garden has already been through the procedure.

I think in terms of age they must have been talking about the girls only as the boys can be much older and perhaps too they meant Mandinka girls in particular as the practice varies from one tribe to another. The tradition is bound up with tribal initiation and coming of age. It involves the appearance of the **Kankurang,** a figure dressed in a mask and clothed in green leaves, bark and natural fibres. Sometimes more than one will appear. Sometimes they will have helpers who are not in costume. A smaller number will sometimes be dressed in red fibre apparel and not the usual brown and green. The Kankurang are at large in the months leading up to the end of the year and during the early period of the New Year. They go about collecting gifts and money for the initiates and are often very intimidating, threatening you with the machetes that they invariably carry. They are key figures in the protection and support of the initiates and the rituals surrounding this (the boys will be away from their parents for some weeks). Apparently they can be found throughout Senegambia. It is also worthy of note that female circumcision when I was in The Gambia was perfectly legal and my later research confirmed that amongst the Mandinka close to 100 per cent of girls undergo this procedure. So too with the Fula but female circumcision is much a minority tradition amongst the Wolof. As far as I could tell male circumcision appears to be universal even amongst predominantly Christian tribes.

In his book *Janjanbureh: A History of an Island Community 1800 – Present*, Foday Jibani Manka, himself a lifelong resident, political representative and elder of this predominantly Mandinka community writes: '... Failing to conform to the norms of the community [an individual] would be severed from his/her roots, his context of security, his kinships and all those who made him/her aware of his/her existence in the community ... In traditional society, circumcision and excision are obligatory social practices that every youth, irrespective of sex, must experience before qualification for entry into adulthood. The *Solimaa* [the uninitiated; the uncircumcised] according to cultural traditions is excluded and forbidden to discover the secrets of the world of adults embodying the moral and spiritual values of traditional society ...'

> A fellow volunteer called Jim, stationed at Basse, has recalled that once whilst on trek on his motorbike he came across a

circumcision event in progress out in the bush. A large number of boys were being systematically circumcised. They were being given a choice of being done by a small medical team or the local blacksmith. Jim remembers that there was a table under a tree for carrying out the procedure. He doesn't recall anything about anaesthetic being available. He remembers seeing a pile of removed foreskins on the ground. Involuntarily I crossed my legs as he recounted his tale.

Today I was explaining to the *kunda* girls that unlike here, where I come from it is not unusual for daughters of their age to answer their fathers back and to decide not to follow their wishes. Hawa Marong's immediate, impassioned and slightly hostile response was 'Why?' It was as if she couldn't imagine any reasonable circumstances under which a daughter's questioning her father's wishes or opinion would be justified. Sometimes it seems to me that our wonderful daughters in the West [and I have three of the very best] find it difficult to imagine circumstances under which they would not!

Today I noticed that baby Sariang, who is now three months old, was sucking at not his mother's breast but his grandmother's, Ndella's. I was told by Jainaba that though Ndella is unable to lactate, this practice is not uncommon here as a means of providing comfort for the child.

Marriage: 'It is a truth universally acknowledged that a man in possession of the means to provide a few bags of rice per month must be in want of at least one wife.' Had Jane Austin been part of the fabric of Janjanbureh society instead of Chawton's she might have begun her most famous tale thus.

I don't know when during my stay in The Gambia it dawned upon me that it was hoped or expected that I would marry one of the unmarried daughters of our compound head but any residual doubts I might have had were dispelled when one day one of them said to me as we sat as a group in my house discussing this and that 'Sariang why is it that you won't marry any of us? Is it because we are black?' The speaker was all of 15 years of age though in appearance would have been taken to be much older by most Westerners. I explained that ethnically mixed marriages were now quite common where I came from but that marriages with such an age disparity were much rarer. My potential brides ranged between fifteen and twenty-three years old – the oldest clearly feeling that by now she had probably missed her opportunity to get married to anyone at all. I was in my early sixties.

The prospect of such a marriage would, by some in my own culture, be frowned upon. There are those who would speak of exploitation and power relations. Further we are often tempted to judge the behaviour of others in our own cultural terms no matter how and where they live. Indeed some will say we have no choice because these are the only standards we have and we must regard them as universal. We do have a choice – we don't have to judge them at all. I explained to the group the kind of reaction I might get from some of my own people were I to enter into such a marriage. With one voice they said they thought such a response would be stupid. Their ability to understand anyone else's way of seeing was no better than ours to understand theirs. Then one said well you don't even have to take us back to the UK you could marry one of us and pay for us to live here in an apartment on the coast and visit when you can.

All I can say is that marriage between twenty year olds and men in their fifties and sixties is quite common in The Gambia. When one of my African office colleagues took his third wife I asked him how old she was. He said he didn't know but that she had completed her school secondary education a couple of years previously. This colleague was fifty-six. I did hear wives complain about their husbands on a variety of grounds which included being beaten, being given insufficient money to keep them and their children etc. or because they weren't very nice people. I never heard any woman complain about their husband on grounds of age.

Further Events, Excursions and People

To Bansang Again:

I motorcycled to Bansang today to get my alien's card renewed. I took the eldest of our compound Hawas with me on the pillion as she was applying for a passport from the customs and immigration office there. Amongst other destinations she has dreams of going to London. I think she didn't let on to her father about the trip as normally she would have to be escorted by someone even to be with me in spite of my age. I was torn between being of service to Hawa and being a party to this deception but on balance agreed. It seemed a shame for her not to be able to take up the offer of a free lift there and back.

Hawa successfully handed in all her documents and is now awaiting the arrival of her passport. I on the other hand was told first that the '2011' rubber stamp needed to issue my new card had not yet arrived. Bansang I was told is merely a provincial office and therefore it might take another month to get there. I was advised to try again in a few weeks. This is worrying as my last card expired in December and I'm not sure what will happen if I'm stopped at one of the many police or army check points on the main highways if I don't have a current alien's card.

Next I was told that perhaps it would be best for me to go to Basse Santa Su, the next and last major town in The Gambia going east before crossing the border into Senegal. It was more likely, I was told, to have received the new stamp. I regard this as a not insignificant journey, especially as they might not have the new stamp anyway.

However finally we learnt that some official from Basse is coming to Janjanbureh tomorrow. It is hoped that I will be able to give him all my application documents and that he will be able to expedite the matter - that is if there is a stamp for him to bring with him. This ad hoc way of muddling through is typical here but can be effective.

On our way back to Janjanbureh our motorbike developed a severe front wheel wobble which I realised only later was caused by a flat tyre. As we progressed we met an oncoming ambulance travelling at high speed with its siren screaming ... on some kind of emergency call. In an attempt to get out of its way I took a line close to the verge and as we entered the ensuing dust cloud caused by the speeding ambulance and visibility was lost I hit the dirt verge. The bike keeled over and we were both pinned beneath it. Fortunately a passing motorist on this sparsely vehicled highway stopped and came to our assistance by pulling the bike off us. By the time he achieved this service the ambulance driver, realising something potentially serious had occurred, also arrived by reversing to the scene of our mishap. After the briefest of checks that we were more or less ok he sped off on his way on his original emergency mission.

I was relieved that Hawa had suffered no serious injury, just a couple of unpleasant grazes, not only because of my concern for her health but also because her father would then have had to be apprised of the circumstances and our unchaperoned trip would have come to light.

We limped home on our barely ridable motorbike still with puncture, both it and ourselves covered in red dust.'

A Koranic Reading

15.01.11: - Between 11am and 2pm, I attended an event to honour, if I understood correctly, the second and most prominent Imam and Alkali of our town after whom Faa Bakari Marong's father and through him myself are named. He was called Sariang Kandeh Jaabi. It was held at the Jaabi family *kunda* which had a large canvas awning especially erected for the occasion. The event was built around two complete readings of the Koran performed by a specialist group of almost forty readers, each of whom was allocated a number of *suras* with all group members reading aloud their allocated *suras* simultaneously. The effect was quite unique with the resulting hum and buzz ultimately forming a single variable kind of drone which I found calming and spiritually engaging. The readings were embedded within a programme that commenced and ended with prayers and included the serving of breakfast, lunch and the passing around of sweets. All present, including me, were dressed in their best African clothes and caps. The women folk were present but gathered together on the other side of a fence erected across the middle of the compound yard in the traditional manner to prevent any visual contact between the two sexes. Our prayers I was informed were to honour the great man himself, the second Imam, our town community and the wider global Islamic community, the ummah. Many of the most prominent town elders were present amongst the approximately one hundred attendees. All, including the women, participated in the prayer responses. I felt strongly how integral is the role of religion and specifically Islam here in binding the community together and in confirming its social structures. It provides an unchanging core and reference point against which everything can be understood. It is hardly surprising that an atheist here is regarded as being at a severe social disadvantage and there is genuine sympathy for such an individual. To be a non-believer here is to be cut off from much of one's own culture, indeed from one's own people.

Presidential Gifts

16.01.11- In contrast to yesterday's more solemn and formal event I was awoken at 2.30am this morning by some very loud music emanating from the police compound in the town situated near the North bank ferry crossing. I had gone to bed before the event really got into swing and assumed that I would be able to sleep through it, being unaware that as time went on the volume of the amplification system would be significantly increased. The party continued for an hour or so after I woke during which time it was impossible to get back to sleep, the power supply in our sector having been extended beyond the usual switch-off time of 2pm so that it could do so.

I have learned that the town has been given five cattle by the President which were slaughtered on the night of 14th of this month and the meat is being distributed to as many people as possible in the town. I am told that this has happened across the country. I wonder whether the fact that we have presidential elections later this year has anything to do with it.

20.01.11 – No electricity at work today as apparently the education office has run out of credit. This continued for some hours before someone went to the local power authority office to buy some more.

The Peace Corps:

I met with some of the local Peace Corps. volunteers in the only bar in town that attracts NGOs in any numbers [called **Bendula**]. The PC volunteers with one exception aren't stationed in our town but rather in the surrounding villages. They will congregate here periodically arriving on foot, by bicycle, by *gelleh-gelleh*, from their placement locations where they normally live singly - Katie, Stephanie, Cat, Evelyn, David, Allison, Erin, Matt, Jen, to name but a few - but on this occasion calamity of calamities - there is no beer to be had in the whole Central River Region since New Year's [when apparently we *toubabs* drank all existent supplies] - the only alcoholic beverages to be had therefore are some spirits e.g. Napoleon Brandy - they come sealed in small plastic sachets and can be almost undrinkable resembling only remotely the spirit they declare themselves to be. They are though 40% proof.

I went to check out the work being done on the accommodation for one of our new volunteers today. She will be in a new terrace being built in a compound which has two other terraces already occupied. The new terrace is still only partly constructed but her house is finished as is the veranda at her end of the terrace. Her pit latrine is the key item currently under construction. So far just a hole about 5ft deep and 3ft in diameter can be seen with no sign of the corrugated iron fence that will create her back yard by separating her bathroom area from its neighbours and the whole terrace of them from the little dirt road running along that side of the compound. Her landlord and Mulai, who is helping to oversee the development, are very pleased with progress so far but to anyone from the developed world facilities seem very basic.

On one occasion some fellow volunteers reported to me that they had arrived home just as their landlord was completing the emptying of their pit latrine. Until this happened I don't think it had ever occurred to any of us volunteers, used as we were to mains sewerage systems back home, that this operation was necessary. But larine pits in our town were not normally sceptic tanks but rather cesspits that required regular and fairly frequent emptying which was accomplished manually, there being none of the relevant mobile and mechanised services available as back home. Thoughtfully landlords like Mulai and my own, always tried to accomplish this unenviable task whilst we were out and without troubling us or indeed without our even knowing it had been done.

I went on **a short trek** on my motorbike to see bits **of the island** outside our township. We will be approaching the hottest time of the year in a couple of months but even now the temperature commonly goes up to the top end of the 30s. I got sunburnt without my hat which I decided to leave at home in case it got blown off my head by the air rush as I rode along. The island is very beautiful and unspoilt. It is typical savannah with scrub, termite mounds and scattered trees including mangoes and palms which abound. There are even a few mahoganies at its western end with growths of thicket and more palms nearer the water's edge. One can walk or ride along the few dirt tracks and usually there is almost no one about. At certain times however one will see small groups of half a dozen to a dozen or so women, their bundles and produce on their heads. They have come from or are returning to the villages on the south bank of the river opposite the island. They follow the track that runs between the town, specifically its market place and the small ferry point at the island's south west tip.

At the eastern end of the island, after disturbing a couple of **red colobus monkeys** which sent them screeching through the undergrowth away from me, I came to a fenced off area which was a banana grove. The man who farmed it was starting his journey back to town along the track down which I had come. He seemed to have many and various items balanced on this head including produce he had harvested and a machete. On my return journey to town I came across two of his sons who were returning to town ahead of him. Oddly I had not seen them earlier on my outward journey. One persuaded me to give him a lift on my pillion seat whilst his brother ran beside us in spite of the great heat. They told me that occasionally, though infrequently, they see **hippos** very early in the morning or very late at night in their father's banana grove. More often however their tracks are the only sign that can be found of the presence of these great beasts. Indeed on and around our island sightings are generally scarce but when they are seen they are to be strictly avoided both on land and in the water. I am told that, if they are around, small craft will not go out into the river until they have gone. They are very dangerous especially when they have young with them and according to my guide book they are responsible for far more premature deaths in Africa that any creature other than the mosquito. There was a notable incident on the River in 2001 when seven people died when a hippo capsized their canoe. Survivors said that the hippo attacked when one of those who were drowned had thrown an orange at it to try to scare it away.

Eventually after dropping off the brothers in town and making a further foray into the island bush, this time in a southerly direction, my motorbike broke down. It was with great effort in the punishing heat that I eventually pushed it back into town. It was a trying end to a pleasant day's excursion. This is the third time I've had a problem with my bike in as many weeks.

Moore records an incident of which he had received a report. Fellow Company employees in a long-boat explained they:

... heard a great noise in the water ... it was a parcel of sea-horses [hippos] ... [we took] ... a gun that was loaded and [fired] among them ... but before the light of the flashing of the pan was out of our eyes ... we got into the midst of them and one of them which was wounded ... flounced and kicked about the boat till ... he knocked a piece out of the bottom of her ... the boat sunk ... poor Mess. Garland and Hayes not knowing how to swim were unfortunately drowned ...

Kuntaur: There have been a couple of treks into the bush recently from my office to check on various schools and to participate as Directorate representatives in their special school events. One such trip was to the Upper Basic School at Kuntaur, a riverside town a little way downstream from Janjanbureh on the north bank of the river.

The event at Kuntaur was arranged to officially receive gifts from a Danish School with which it has a long standing link, some of whose staff and students had made a special trip from Denmark to be there.

European links with Kuntaur have a long and note-worthy history. They stretch back to the 15th century when this fabled settlement was known by Europeans as 'Cantor'. Then this port and market town was a major centre for trade in gold and other commodities that had come down the river from deeper in the interior. Its reputation had reached Europeans long before they ventured here. Stories of Cantor had travelled across the Maghreb via the trade routes to Ceuta on the southern shores of the Mediterranean. The Portuguese sailed up the Gambia to Cantor in the 1450s. It was the farthest point navigable up-river for vessels of any size, there being a draft of some 150ft. The Portuguese were keen to gather information especially about the gold coming down from the headwaters of the Senegal and Niger rivers, from Timbuktu and from elsewhere. Then and in the years that followed they conducted a thriving trade in gold and much else including slaves. To secure this trade they had to negotiate peaceful passage with the various African chiefs along the route to Cantor from the coast.

The gifts from the Danes were in the form of school materials. There were speeches, an appearance by the Kankurang, faceless in his usual garb of orange tree bark and fibres finished with fleshy laurel-like leaves, dancing frenetically and tirelessly in time to some improvised percussion and a school whistle. Later we were entertained by a scout band with mainly drums and a few bugles and other instruments. The event culminated in a speech made by **Amat my Directorate colleague** with whom I had made the trip. His role was to give greater gravitas to the proceedings; to bring the blessing of a higher authority to the event. He stood up to speak and formally welcomed the overseas visitors, thanked them for their gifts and went on to give an account of his own earlier happy experiences at the school as a senior staff member. His speech was delivered in his favourite headgear at that time, a child's **cowboy hat**. I thought of the illustrious history of the town, of its trade in gold but also wondered what the Danes made of it all as Amat got into full flow with

Amat Bah sans his child's cowboy hat

his cowboy hat rocking backwards and forwards and sometimes from side to side.

Another trip took us to **Sere Babou** Basic Cycle School to open a new teaching block. We arrived in our small trucks via barely discernible tracks through the bush. The community here is essentially Fulah. There was a wonderful band with a crude fiddle-like bowed instrument as well as many drums to start proceedings. We were given Baobab juice and much food, the ingredients of which I was unable to identify. There were more speeches and prayers led by the Imam who was very welcoming. The local housing was very traditional mainly round in shape with adobe walls and grass roofs. As ever the children were fascinated by my European appearance. I was in full African dress including a Muslim style pill box hat.

An older boy visiting the compound killed our proudest cockerel today after many of our children had chased it down. Efo, the young girl who usually sweeps and cleans my house, managed to grab its legs finally after it ran into the house next to mine and it became cornered. She was very pleased with herself and came to tell me of her achievement. It was the best looking and proudest of the current brood of chickens in our compound with magnificent plumage around head, neck and wings that glistened radiantly in the sunlight as it strutted about its business sometimes flapping its wings widely in a display. Some of the brood are almost naked, their feathers having fallen victim to the attacks of some of their more pugilistic brothers and sisters. This bird was identified as Baby Sariang's cockerel, the baby named after me. Once handed over to him the older boy unemotionally pinned the bird to the ground by standing with a foot on each of its glossy, translucent, shiny blue-green wings so that its head was pinned against the ground. With a machete he delivered calmly a short, downward thrust to its neck and waited for its blood and life to drain away into the red dust. I assume he whispered a prayer in the Islamic way but this was inaudible to me. In The Gambia almost everyone is sometimes a slaughter man.

National Elections are coming!

A lorry load of the President's supporters came into the town today making lots of noise. I wasn't sure whether this was in aid of a special political event or an early start to their campaign. Elections are not being held until November. I wondered whether the opposition are ever able to disport themselves in this way without some sort of official reaction!

This was the second time during my stay on the island that I experienced a visit to our township from the supporters of the APRC [Alliance for Patriotic Reorientation and Construction] the President's and of course the dominant, party in the country. The first visit was from the female activist wing some months earlier. They arrived with no warning and much noise in a couple of coaches chanting party slogans. These women were dressed from head to foot in flowing African dresses and head wraps which depicted large smiling images of the President. They came with a swagger and an arrogance, were formidable and not a little intimidating. Our directorate office campus was their first port of call in the town. All Directorate staff who lived on site in the residential blocks, with the exception of the Regional Director, were summarily evicted. Colleagues found whatever alternative accommodation they could which usually meant sleeping on the floor of the house of any colleague who happened to live in town beyond the campus. No one either resisted or questioned having to do this and as far as I know no one complained to anyone about what had happened subsequently. This would have been regarded as a distinct risk. You don't question the Big Man or his supporters.

Further Sad News:

'Baks' [Bakari], our friendly barman at Bendula [our favourite local bar] and his wife have just lost their first baby. He/she was still born. I wasn't able to establish the detailed circumstances - a very sad business of which we volunteers might have remained ignorant had not one of his African 'brothers' informed us of the event. I gave him my deepest sympathies.

In 2009 the stillbirth rate in The Gambia was approximately 7.5 times higher than in the UK.

Birthdays:

Asked Efo, who is 12 years old and lives in my compound, to tell me the date of her birthday. She couldn't – she only knows the year in which she was born. She is from a poorer wing of our compound family. Her own more immediate family have a dilapidated compound elsewhere in our town. I tried the same thing with Hawa Jallow who is 15 and who is a member of the better-off family which owns our compound – same result. Mostly they speak of how many rains they have seen rather than of years or specific dates.

To the Coast Once More

It is early February and I am off to the Kombos again. My NGO has summoned our cohort of volunteers back to HQ to undergo a progress review and to meet a few further additional administrative demands.

Friday 6.00am and I make my way to the ferry point. The town sleeps but not without its stirrings and murmurings. A dog coughs, a solitary woman bends at the waist in the African manner, to reach her small brazier that her men folk use for the brewing of *ataya*. She empties out yesterday's ashes. It is quiet enough for the light breeze to rattle audibly the corrugated sheeting. It is liberally used in the town for constructing enclosures, roofs and much else. A battered old *gelleh-gelleh* throbs into life at the beginning of another day of operating at the edge of its functionality.

I cross the river by the small ferry and am able to catch the first Peugeot sept-place of the day to depart going west. It leaves for the coast along the North Bank Road once all its seats have been taken. The state of the vehicle and the fact that the driver, as they all do, insists that three passengers occupy the two seats in the third and back row guarantees discomfort for all.

Check Points: In no time we come to a halt at one of the many check points. As I think I have remarked before, The Gambia must be one of the most controlled plots of land on earth. There are a remarkable number of check points and police, customs, immigration and military personnel for such a small country. Military check points are usually set up on a road at the point at which it runs past a military camp. They will be manned by helmeted, gun-toting soldiers and often have back up from a machine gun emplacement to one side of the road. They will have a gunner lying on his stomach, trigger poised, his aim trained directly at you with gun barrel poking through a wall of sandbags and camouflage netting. As an occupant of a stopped vehicle this is disconcerting. You hope the sun or some other circumstance hasn't addled his brain to the point where he might do the wrong thing.

Police check points can usually be safely negotiated by a pleasant smile and handshake and by a small offering of a nan [small plastic bag of fresh water] or other small gift to help the officer through the day but sometimes inconveniently, searches are carried out with rigour and items are confiscated.

One is warned never to photograph passing soldiers or uniformed personnel, prisons or indeed military establishments for this is a country of great political and military paranoia. Politically positive opinions of the President, his largesse and the state of the current economy are commonly met with. Counter views are not and people will only share them with you, in confidence, if they feel that you constitute no danger of transmitting their authorship to the wrong people.

Up-Country Again

13.02.11: Went to **Bansang RC Church** for Communion today. This was my second visit. I must say that of all the church visits I have made since arriving here those made to this church are the only ones that have induced a feeling one might describe as spiritual. To get there I travel by motorcycle for approximately half an hour along the South Bank Road which is really only a dirt and sand road through the bush – plans for its remaking and tarmacking are taking an inordinately long time to implement. The effort of the journey will often give me a feeling of pilgrimage and penitence which puts me in the right state of mind for the service.

The priest officiating introduced himself to me as Stanislaus. I asked him if he was Father Stanislaus – 'No' he said and proceeded to tell me that he was in fact a deacon and not yet finally ordained. This did not stop him from celebrating the Eucharist in one kind during the service. I was glad to receive it having not been able to do so elsewhere since my return to Africa. I discovered later that the deacon's apparent celebration of the sacrament was not a local and unilateral decision taken to dispense with Church protocol but rather that this arrangement had been legitimised by some changes to the liturgy and by the host having been consecrated in advance by the absent priest.

Like most up-country churches I have visited, this one is very basic in its construction and interior appurtenances. There are benches which are usually very dusty with a wooden cross nailed to the wall above the holy altar. I noticed too, which I had not really been conscious of on my earlier visit, that the picture of the Madonna and Child above the altar to the left featured a black Virgin and infant Jesus whereas the picture of the mature Jesus with outstretched arms and bleeding heart to the right is a more standard, bearded Caucasian looking white figure. I was glad I had not really registered this inconsistency before – it played no part in the

A Kankurang with machete in hand

A Dancing Kankurang

expression of the overriding themes intended by this iconography including those of love, innocence and compassion.

On my return home I encountered **a troop of monkeys** along the road about fifty strong. They scattered on my approach in several directions but a few of their 'sentries' watching from behind trees or from the tops of hillocks stood their ground so as to track my progress as I passed. When you look at the arid landscape at this time of year well into the dry season, you really wonder what they find to eat to see them through to the rains in June.

Initiation event Janjanbureh:

19.02.11: We are currently still in the **Kankurang Festival** period – the Mandinka tradition confirming tribal membership and celebrating a key stage in the passage to adulthood. At this time you are likely to encounter individuals or small groups of costumed figures called *Kankurangs* going about their business as protectors, teachers and guides of the newly initiated.

The new boy circumcisees return to their families with Kankurang support

Today I went to a well-attended event to mark the return of the latest batch of initiates to their families. It involved a group of a dozen or so male initiates probably 6 to 8 years old. They were being returned to their families after an absence of some weeks at bush school during which they had been circumcised and the sacred mysteries of their tribe had been revealed to them. They wore full length white hooded robes and face masks so that their identities were not revealed until the right moment which was the high point of the proceedings. Once the masks were removed the boys squatted on all fours in pairs on a sheet and were given money. Their compound and extended families had come to this large open space on the edge of town, dominated by a small number of giant and ancient baobabs, dressed in their finest clothes with the women of the same family all in identical outfits. They represented the home team so to speak of their own returning little boy who was now older, wiser and a fuller community member. Only the women came forward to receive each of them back into their own particular family fold.

Until that point the antics of a group of five or six *Kankurang* figures had taken centre stage in their garb of orange fibre, bark and leaves of the faara tree and with a machete in each hand - except for one who was a figure entirely dressed in red fibres, also armed with machetes. I think he is called the *Nefere*. Having made the mistake of photographing the proceedings I was sought out by this group from amongst the crowd of many hundreds, surrounded by them and threatened quite graphically until I made a financial contribution to their fund which they were collecting to support the initiates and the proceedings generally.

Once returned to their families the initiates were processed with great fanfare into the centre of town to a point close to the Chief's *kunda*. Here there was much dancing and drumming accompanied by sport's whistles. Finally the initiates were borne off shoulder high each by his family to his own *kunda*.

Francis Moore reports that:

... some short time before the rainy season begins they circumcise a great number of boys about twelve or fourteen years of age after which they put on a peculiar habit ... from the time of their circumcision to the time of the rains they are allowed to commit what outrage they please without being called to account for it.

27.02.11: **On trek** for the second day running today. Went to one school where there were a lot of **tsetse flies** buzzing around in the head teacher's office. First time I've seen my colleague Amat worried about anything in the natural environment. He was of course concerned about contracting sleeping sickness but also about the painfulness of the bite itself. The school staff said this was a problem with the school location and that these flies were often about. Somehow however they seemed more relaxed than Amat about the situation and a little amused at his timidity. Someone said they thought that a special strain of the fly had been bred that was incapable of carrying the disease and it had been integrated into the main tsetse fly population. Certainly according to my guide book the disease is now rare in this part of West Africa although there remains a risk. Apparently the tsetse fly is attracted to large moving objects [e.g. cows, trucks, boats] and to dark clothing - its favourite colour is said to be blue. Like Amat I took no chances and was unable to relax fully until we had left the head teacher's office.

A little later in the year during a sightseeing trip in a pirogue down the Gambia River I suddenly became aware that we were being tracked a couple of feet above our heads by a tsetse fly. Our African pilot on that occasion was most wary of the insect. However I managed to get in a lucky swat at it with my bush hat and condemned it to a watery grave to everyone's relief.

The treatment of animals:

The view that generally animals are not best treated here in West Africa is not uncommon amongst visitors and indeed by western standards it is difficult to escape this conclusion. For example one sees countless live chickens ignominiously hanging from bicycle handlebars with their feet bound and live goats and sheep tied to the tops of long distance buses and *gelleh-gellehs* sometimes uncomfortably positioned in relation to roof bars etc. Once, just before *Tobaski*[Gambian name for Eid al-Adha], I saw two rams sitting passively in the boot of a car that could barely accommodate them whilst a third was just being forced into the same space. I have no idea whether the driver intended to close the boot lid for the journey itself or not but it wouldn't have surprised me. On another occasion I saw three sheep being wheeled off the Barra Ferry in a wheelbarrow - indeed such as this is a totally unremarkable sight. Further I have seen goats strapped on their flanks to the small rectangular carrier above the rear wheel of a bicycle – you would hardly think it possible. Commonly too, drivers make few concessions to animals wandering across the road in front of them. I have seen a number of goats and sheep run over and hobble away with an injury, frequently a broken leg. In such circumstances their owner might simply tape up their damaged leg with whatever sticky tape or string comes to hand. I don't know whether there are any vets here. Today however we passed a most peculiar scene whilst out on trek in one of our vehicles. It seemed to me the ultimate indignity. A donkey had been strapped down on its flank inside its own cart with its unsupported head lolling over the tailboard. Even my African colleagues thought this was a bit rich and showed some interest in what was happening though I wouldn't call it alarm or indignation. When I asked them what they thought was the purpose of doing this, they said they thought the intention probably was to hook-up the cart to a car or truck, so that both the donkey and its cart could be moved a long distance much more quickly than if it tried to do the same journey under its own steam.

Family relationships and internal slavery:

Efo [a diminutive for Fatima] is approximately 12 years old and she lives in my *kunda*. She was here at the beginning of January when I returned from the UK although she had not been here when I left to go there. I am getting to know her well as she has made herself responsible for cleaning my house. She is not, if I have understood correctly, a member of the nuclear family which lives in and owns my compound but is a relative from either Faa Bakari's or Ndella's extended family. I asked Efo recently where her immediate family lives and she said here in our town. I found this perplexing and wondered why she didn't live in her own family compound. However ever since I have arrived here in West Africa I have become more and more aware of a certain fluidity in the membership of the family and compound groups in which people live which I don't fully understand. Regarding my own *kunda*, relationships have been a mystery to me. This lack of clarity has been further compounded not just by comings and goings but by a different use of terminology in English. The terms 'brother' and 'sister' are not used here as narrowly as most of us use them in the literal sense in England to indicate common parentage but can apply to much more genetically distant relationships or simply to close friends or those with whom you share your *kunda*. You will be pleased to know for example that I have many brothers and sisters here. Frequently too there can be a wide divergence in age between siblings from the same father so that it isn't always easy to guess correctly in which strata of descent an individual is located in relation to a senior male family member. In my *kunda* several of the young women I took originally to be sisters in our sense, self-proclaimed as such as they were, turn out to be variously one another's aunt, niece, cousin and in one case mother of two of the others who are half-sisters.

Efo has an older brother and sister here who lived with us before she arrived.

Today a small framed, slender and quite old looking man with a weather-beaten face dressed in a torn and dirty haftan came into our *kunda*. He bought some fish with him in a small pail which he gave to our women folk. He didn't stay long and as far as I could see no money changed hands. After he had left Efo told me that this was her father. She said he was a fisherman and that he fishes alone from a dugout canoe on the River. 'We are poor' she said. I was initially surprised to learn that this visitor was Efo's father because whilst he was present I hadn't noticed any special acknowledgement by either of them towards the other. I wondered momentarily why Efo hadn't run up to him and exchanged an embrace and perhaps a kiss. Was she ashamed of him? Were they estranged for one reason or another? But then I remembered that this was to assume far too much. I had forgotten what I had already learnt since I've been here that displays of tactile affection don't happen between genders in public, not even between those so closely related as Efo and her father, unless one party is still in infancy. There might well have been more subtle acknowledgements operating between them which fell far below my ability to pick up on them.

On a subsequent occasion I noticed amidst the life in the yard of our *kunda* which on this particular evening continued much later into the night than usual, the time was about 11pm, there was an old lady with her flat iron charged with glowing charcoals trying to get through a great pile of freshly washed and dried clothes. The night was hot and uncomfortable and draining of one's energy. I felt sorry that she was working so late. I think the idea was that as the washing had been done by our own *kunda* women earlier that day a special effort was now being made to complete its processing and she had been brought in especially to help with this task. I felt guilty when she presented herself at my door with a pile of a dozen and a half of my own shirts that she had just completed. I had forgotten that I had generated my fair share of the work. She stood in my doorway with her thin, wrinkled and worn features and smiled a broad smile revealing her decayed brown and black teeth and the gaps between them with headscarf still correctly in place and its bow erect on her head. She passed the shirts to me. They were unbearably hot even to hold briefly and especially on such a sweltering night. I thanked her and she left. Efo told me later that this woman was her mother. I could not quite believe that any woman of her aged and worn appearance could have given birth as recently as only twelve years previously – life seemed to have drained her so completely of almost every vestige of youthfulness.

A recent conversation with **a local historian** here who is the elected representative for our town at the National Assembly in Banjul and who is a life-long resident, namely **Foday Manka**, has perhaps filled in a few gaps in my understanding of all this. He has just completed a history of the town and is letting me have a copy of the first few to be printed. In the course of our discussions he mentioned what he called 'in-

ternal slavery'. He told me that it is not uncommon across West Africa for some low status Africans to be virtual slaves to better off families – this internal slavery he says has always existed and will transfer from one generation to another. It is at least partly self-imposed. I am beginning to think that Efo's nuclear family, poorer members of the extended family, have this relationship with the principal nuclear family that lives in and owns my compound though this has not been obvious to me through their behaviour because all the women here work hard. If difference in status is sometimes implied within compound discourse and chatter this would be hard for me to detect as this is always conducted through tribal languages with which I have never got to grips. However I think that I have noticed that less care is taken in ensuring that chaperoning arrangements occur correctly in relation to male outsiders with the girls from the poorer wing of the family than with the others.

... Some people have a good many house slaves which is their greatest glory and they live so well and easy that it is sometimes a very hard matter to know the slaves from their masters and mistresses ...
writes Moore.

More widely here and perhaps unsurprisingly just as elsewhere, perceived status seems to be an important issue. At the Directorate for example there is some evidence that when a new school has been provided to meet the needs of a cluster of villages within our region then if it is located within a village that is regarded as low status the attendance from the children from other villages especially those from higher status villages will be affected and be less good.

Kora Concert, Independence Day, another Koranic Reading and the Slaughter of the Bulls

This has been for a variety of reasons a crowded weekend. On Friday night, commencing at approximately midnight a kora singer and his band gave a concert at what was referred to as the community centre. This was basically a compound perimeter wall forming an enclosure but with no buildings inside. The amplification was turned up so loud that the speakers couldn't quite handle it and the music became distorted. In spite of this the musicians proved themselves to be very skilful.

The following day, Saturday, was **Independence Day** and in the morning there was a march-past at the sports field opposite Armitage Senior Secondary School involving the police, the army, the fire brigade and several other organisations followed by each local school with children in their uniforms. The salute was taken by the Governor of the Central River Region and there were many dignitaries with their wives all dressed in their finest clothes. Apparently there was an official reception later on, which we missed due to confusion over timing – should we have expected anything else?

Further, all weekend in my own compound, there have been 40 or 50 women preparing food for another Koran reading scheduled for Sunday, this time to celebrate our late Marong compound grandfather, my namesake Sariang Marong.

For this event **two bulls** had been purchased by Faa Bakari. They had lived with us in our compound for a few days leading up to the weekend and I had been told that they were to be slaughtered in the compound. This was an event to which I was not looking forward, not only because I am unused to witnessing such things but especially because they were such magnificent beasts with their great long, imperious horns and their smooth coats that glistened with a deep and subtle luminosity. On Saturday night when I went to bed at a late hour, they remained in life and I almost held out the hope for them that their fate had somehow been altered. When I awoke however I saw Faa Bakari and some other men squatting around two very large, garishly coloured, plastic tubs. One containing the most grotesque melange of animal body parts with stomach linings [I think!] that looked like coconut matting and various other entrails and innards; the other with cuts of meat and offal that looked considerably more edible. I knew that as a food source both of these tubs would be fully utilised by my African hosts. When I enquired as to when, how and where this transformation of these beautiful animals had occurred Faa Bakari explained that the slaughter men had arrived in darkness, in fact at around 4am to carry out their grim task. I imagined now the scene as it unfolded with first one proud bull being forced onto its flank by leverage applied though its wonderful horns, its feet tied together and the animal dispatched whilst the other stood tethered just a few feet away awaiting its turn.

Soon I was presented with a plastic bag full of meat for my own consumption especially chosen for me as a honoured compound resident. However not being able to identify which bits of the unfortunate animals they were and possessing only a two ringed gas hob, I persuaded one of our *kunda* girls to add my gift to the meat that was being cooked on the wood fires in the compound for the feeding of the guests generally.

No sooner had this reading of the Koran taken place and the guests dispersed than I was told of a further event in the town to celebrate the return of another batch of circumcisees from bush school. Indeed the **Kankurang** had visited our compound early this morning with flailing machetes frightening

A *Nefere Kankurang* visits our compound

the women and children on his mission to collect money. With conflicting emotions on their part some of the women, namely Fatou and Jainaba, were manhandled by this costumed apparition. They seemed not to know whether to be fearful or laugh. I stepped forward and offered the Kankurang ten dalasi to leave us alone and withdraw which thankfully he did.

The heat:

12.03.11. There has been a steady increase in temperature each day this week. My thermometer today was showing 45°c at one point. According to my guide book during this month and the next we can expect the highest yearly average temperatures.

Francis Moore tells us that:

... the most excessive heat is reckoned to be generally the latter end of May a fortnight or three weeks before the rainy season ...

He did not have the benefit of carefully logged meteorological data to underpin this report no doubt but my experience up-country confirms that temperatures from March to May not unusually reach the mid-40s. When I came here a volunteer colleague told me that 50°c was not unknown. When I put this to my office companion Amat he explained that this happens but only very rarely which it did a couple of years ago. He said sometimes birds would fall out of the sky because they were so dehydrated. Alpha our PEO recalls that when he was in Basse, almost always hotter by two or three degrees than our town as it's further inland [and before they got air-conditioning] the Directorate staff could never stay in their offices after around midday in the hot season and would move their desks outside to the nearest tree that offered some reasonable degree of shade.

Fund Raising Event:

17.03.15. Today we attended the Methodist School fund raising event in the community centre compound. There was a dance competition which was won by Mama, the 8 year old from our compound. She really is very good with a natural sense of timing and of style. Her mother Fatou also has a reputation as an accomplished dancer apparently and Mama won by unanimous consent. Then we had a Wolof magician who danced on broken glass, had his face pushed into broken glass and finally had a wood fire built on his chest surmounted by a pot in which an omelette was cooked. The omelette was then served to some of the audience in the front row as proof that it was indeed cooked. There followed some Jola stilt dancers in traditional tribal festival masks and costumes who were mounted on impossibly high stilts.

Safo:

Today two of our girls spent some time explaining to me their special charms or fetishes [not to be misunderstood in any alternative contemporary sense!] which are worn almost universally here up-country. They are called *safo* in Mandinka and *teere* in Wolof if I understood correctly [not *gris-gris* as in some parts of West Africa]. They consist of small leather or cloth pouches suspended from a leather thong worn around the neck, wrist, waist or ankle. When I asked what they contain they said usually the protuberance or spur from just above a goat's hoof. I noticed that when Baby Sariang was born he was, in a matter of days, supplied with one of these. They are said to bring good luck and to guard against evil spirits and no one seems to feel any conflict between their belief in the power of these fetishes and their Islamic faith. Time and again one is confronted with evidence that the old Animism is alive and well and too deeply rooted for modernity or any overlaid religious code to dislodge.

Rats!

I have been told by one of my fellow volunteers in our town, who goes by the name of Sankumba, that he woke up to find a rat in his bedroom scratching at the furniture. He thought it must have come through a hole he has found in the window fly-screen. When he reported this to his compound landlord thinking something might be done the latter simply reported that he had himself recently found two dead rats under his own bed. And again another colleague reports that he had a rat in his house. His landlord cornered it and eventually managed to kill it by pushing a stick through its head. And again a Peace Corps friend Katie, who lives just across the river in a village near the ferry terminal at Lamin Koto tells me she returned home to her adobe hut to find no less than five rats installed. They left casually by climbing a roof support pole and disappeared through a hole at the top, just above her bed, which gave entry to the roof structure. I elicited these stories when I mentioned that I had heard what I took to be something, probably a rat, in the night scratching at my window. I heard a crash and then scampering in my back yard. In the morning I discovered that my solar torch had been knocked off my outside window ledge where I had left it earlier that day in the sunshine to recharge. I am hoping that rats don't eventually manage to penetrate my house defences but there is every possibility that they will. When one sleeps here one is never quite at ease.

Moore writes:

... In one corner of my room I have a large jar of water raised upon 'forkillas' to keep it from vermin ...

The Lumo:

Went to Brikamaba lumo [market] today – it was very hot and crowded as usual. I took Sankumba on the back of my motorbike. Tida, another volunteer colleague, followed on hers. [We regularly address and refer to one another using our African given names even when no Africans are present – it might be interesting sometime to consider why]. On the return journey Tida got a puncture just as we passed through a village called Fula Bantang. It took three hours to repair at a local friendly compound which not only carried out the work for us but supplied us with lunch consisting of fish balls, vegetables and the inevitable rice and plenty of water from their well. This level of hospitality here is always impressive even though one comes across it so often. I was careful to identify the compound leader and thanked him profusely for all their help. Additionally we gave them 100 dalasi for their trouble – with which they seemed quite content.

It was Palm Sunday today and I went to the R.C. church at Bansang. They held the usual procession as witness to Christ's entry into Jerusalem. There were crosses made with local fresh palm leaves picked only this morning. Father Peter has returned following a prolonged absence spent on the coast with treatment for eye problems. Although she was not present on this occasion I will sometimes take Joanna on my pillion – she is a very pleasant and polished Peace Corps volunteer and a practising Roman Catholic from Washington DC.

Today some of our *kunda* girls and their friends came and gave me the best cleaning job ever with everything including my outside bathroom – including its walls and floor – as well as my small outside yard, scrubbed. Additionally my house was thoroughly swept and the floor washed. Even the fly-screens were dusted. To cap it all a large, decorated, earthenware incense burner was brought in to make everything smell fresher. Once installed the window and door curtains were shut to ensure the fragrance was unable to escape easily before it could permeate everything. This *turai* with its much more superior incense than my joss-sticks does not usually inflame my asthma as they do.

It was around this point that in correspondence with my NGO **I agreed to extend my placement beyond this summer** for an indefinite period of up to a year feeling there was more to be done.

Bin Laden is Dead!

03.05.11: A shocking morning! Whilst following my daily routine – making my porridge around 7am after my shower and shave and listening to the BBC African World Service – I learnt that Osama Bin Laden has been found and killed in Pakistan by US Special Forces. I think because he'd been sought for so long one began to think it would never happen.

I had encountered some evidence of Muslim solidarity here since my arrival and the phrase 'Remember you are a Muslim' was one that a senior colleague had used more than once in my presence to try to encourage correct and brotherly behaviour between individual colleagues. I wondered how deeply this went and peered out of my window just in case a hostile mob was gathering in my compound yard with retribution on its mind. There are but a few Westerners here and Brits do have a global reputation for being America's ally. I was relieved when I saw nothing to disturb the sluggish life in the yard which was following its inexorable course and could hear no distant commotion such as might be generated by an approaching mob.

At work I raised the news of Bin Laden's death with an African colleague whose only response was, 'Well if you behave like Bin Laden then that's what you can expect'. I felt relieved but remained a little on my guard for the rest of the morning. Perceptions of world events are not always the same here as back home as one might imagine.

Our NGO has remained silent on the Bin Laden killing and we have received no advice of any kind from them. Fellow Peace Corps volunteers who are stationed singly in the surrounding villages tell me that they have been told to remain vigilant and to travel in twos if at all possible.

Snake: Saw a five foot snake opposite the prison a couple of days ago. I would estimate that it was approximately an inch and a half in diameter – perhaps a little more. Someone ran up to it and tried to kill it with a brick but they missed and it made its escape into the undergrowth. When I mentioned this to a colleague he said that our Regional Director has lost two sheep recently and one theory was that this was a consequence of snake bite.

I saw another, smaller snake, a month or so ago which had been killed by some local boys.

17.05.11 - It rained for the first time this year in our town last night and I fell asleep with it drumming on the corrugated roof of my house. This is earlier than expected as the rainy season does not really get underway until mid-June usually. I am told that it's likely that we won't get any serious downpours until then.

I continue to be struck by the differences between the typical palates of my African hosts and our own tastes in the UK The amount of sugar people eat here is quite shocking. They will put three heaped dessertspoons full of sugar in a cup of coffee, a drink which is not however particularly commonly drunk here. They have no concept of enjoying the bitterness of coffee. However their green tea or *ataya* gets the same treatment.

Rice as I have mentioned constitutes the bulk of anyone's diet. It is eaten three times a day - if three meals are indeed taken - and seven days a week. For breakfast it is usually eaten as porridge with the rice pounded together with groundnuts. Sugar is then added with milk powder, if they have it. When they have fresh milk, which one tends to come across only out in the villages, it is often preferred when it is beginning to turn sour.

As far as I can see there is no difference between lunch and dinner in terms of the type of food prepared and indeed dinner is frequently the remains of the lunchtime cooking effort. Meals will feature large quantities of rice with very small quantities of fish or meat and vegetables - if indeed there is any of this. Commonly the rice is eaten with just a sauce.

The weather here is now very challenging. Daytime temperatures are almost always very high and sometimes this continues right into the evening and night-time. As we approach more closely the wet season the atmosphere becomes more humid. I sit in my house with arms covered in sweat especially where they come into contact with the arms of my chair and with my shirt stuck to my back. When we lose power between 4pm and 7pm I sit outside as it is too hot to stay inside with no fan. Recently too the power supply has been erratic and sometimes the late afternoon to early evening power gap has been extended to conserve power with it not returning until 11pm.

I feel as if I could do with a break from all this and need to spend some time back in the UK to recover my strength and willpower before the start of the next school year in September. Then things at work will become pretty hectic as they did last year with new postings settling down, vacancies being filled and resource issues to be dealt with generally.

Last night one of our local Peace Corps volunteers came for an overnight stay. She was coming through Janjanbureh to catch a lift with a PC vehicle on its way to the Kombos. It was coming down from Basse further up-river. She is an Irish American from Maine and is based at Wassu just north of the river. We had no power until 11pm so we sat outside by candlelight and talked, drank tea and water and both felt too hot to eat. I gave her a lift on my motorbike early this morning across the bridge at the southern tip of our island to her rendezvous point on the South Bank Road.

The gem in **the landscape** here is the river. Whenever I see it I am struck by its great beauty. The same cannot be said of much of the rest of the landscape at this time of year. Going on trek to the rural schools as I do frequently I see plenty of it. The terrain is flat with scattered scrub, trees and grass. It is dry and dead mostly and although some plant life persists in its green state throughout the hot season it still has a deadness and inert quality about it that somehow inspires in me a spiritual malaise. Mainly too one sees very little animal life – that is except for the village cattle which always look splendid with their long, handlebar horns, the feral domestic dogs and the sheep and goats – but nothing wild – just the occasional monkey or family of baboons.

The earth is red and the rural tracks unforgiving. In the dry season our vehicles are constantly jolted as we travel down them with the occasional area of soft sand – these latter presenting a particular problem for our motorbikes. However, especially along the North Bank Road, whatever the time of year, at certain points one encounters unexpectedly areas of **exotic palms with lily-padded pools** set in marshland. These watering places act as magnets for cattle and therefore for the white, yellow-billed egrets which will attach themselves to their backs and sift and probe the ground, swamp and pools around their feet. With such exceptions of landscape it can be hard at this time of year to see much beauty in this seriously inhospitable terrain.

Corruption?: Today we, that is to say most of the professional staff complement at the Directorate office, the ones who go on trek, have been asked to sign in advance for re-

Lily-padded pool on the North Bank Road

ceipt of an 'on trek' allowance to which we are entitled but of which we have been told we will receive a lesser payment than that signed for. One immediately suspected some sort of corrupt practice. This did after all amount to a falsification of the records. The Regional Director explained that he was asking us to do this so that he could distribute the allowance pot more widely to include those who work at the regional office but who are not officially entitled to any such payment as they don't actually go out on-trek. However we have no way of knowing whether the total pot available will be distributed as claimed or indeed how much it is in total. In any case this had created some discord as there are those who feel that they should be paid the full allowance to which they personally are entitled.

The volunteers as one body have refused to sign as has a least one of our senior African officer colleagues.

And later:

We have now signed for the allowance payment as assurance has been received via a senior officer sent by the Regional Director that the sum we will receive will in fact be equal to that signed for. I did so with some reluctance as I could not understand why we were signing now instead of at the time we actually get paid as we do with our regular salary [which always arrives in the form of cash with a paymaster from Banjul who is accompanied by two heavily armed guards, most employees not having bank accounts and indeed with only a very limited number of local banks and branches scattered around the country].

Later we were told that we had misunderstood what we had been told on this last occasion and that the amount to be received would indeed be less than that for which we had signed. We therefore asked for a meeting with the Regional Director and at the appointed time presented ourselves at his house. On behalf of fellow dissenters I explained that we were not prepared to present a false picture to the consumers of the official document in question, indeed effectively the Ministry of Education in Banjul and told him that we wished to officially withdraw our signatures. At this point the Regional Director agreed and produced a different sheet for us to sign with the correct figures that on his direct assurance he said did represent the true smaller amount that we would actually be paid. We duly signed this new document, which already contained other signatures, but when I asked for the original sheet we had signed to be given to us so that we could destroy it he claimed it had already been burnt. As we were unable to verify this we were at a loss as to know what else we could do and left feeling that we had probably lost control over what return would finally be submitted to the Ministry in Banjul. We have been warned before arriving at our placements that we might encounter corrupt practices during the course of our work. We could not be sure whether this was an example or not.

I must admit now to having lost a degree of confidence in **our Regional Director** because initially I had been quite impressed by his quiet and apparently self-assured demeanour. But when he is here which is infrequently he seems to be determined not to consider changing anything and not to consult others even though we are blessed with **a very highly motivated and dynamic PEO, Alpha Camara**, who came to us with an excellent reputation for progress from a directorate further upriver. Neither this PEO nor I in my role as Directorate Advisor have been encouraged to participate in reviewing the major work practices and strategies of the Directorate nor have we been consulted meaningfully in any key decision making. It was perhaps indicative of things to come when I discovered earlier on, after the event, that the Regional Director had called a meeting of senior Directorate staff on the eve of the new PEO's arrival at which, by report, he told those present not to follow any instructions except his own and their own judgements. It was of note that I was not invited to this meeting nor indeed even notified of its taking place. I can only think that this was generated by a deep seated fear that his authority might be undermined by the new PEO and by me for which there is not the slightest foundation. Indeed this was partly suggested to me later again when in response to a request received by the Regional Director from the PEO for him, the PEO and me to share an office so that we could work more closely together whilst I continue here, so that he might benefit from my experience, this was flatly turned down by the Regional Director. This kind of experience sharing is after all is a key purpose of my placement.

Moore's position was not without its frustrations. To his RAC superiors at James Fort he writes in a letter from Brucoe:

> ... I am sorry you have debarred me from trading with the Portuguese because I am certain it will be a loss to the Company there being as much trade to be made with them as with the Mundingoes ... you have given me such positive orders that I am resolved not to trade with them but sooner than they will sell their wax [bees-wax] and teeth [ivory] to me for the prices you mentioned they will carry it down to the separate [independent] traders and sell it for a greater.
>
> I am surprised you have debarred me from taking any iron or any other heads of money to diet account [to vire any surpluses across to the food account] ... because it is impossible to buy provisions without it and unless you will please to allow it we must either starve or be obliged to leave the factory ...

Scorpions: I met a Swede from another NGO, FIOH [Future in Our Hands] who said that a female colleague in his organisation has had to return to Sweden for treatment because she had been stung by a scorpion and became quite ill. Apparently her liver has been affected.

This is the first time I have heard of such an occurrence since I have been here and it has prompted me to ask others if they know of similar instances. We never see scorpions at all although the guide books tell us that they are everywhere.

One volunteer within our own organisation in Basse reported that they had seen a scorpion as did another in Soma. My enquiries with African colleagues resulted in a report from one that he had seen one recently, for the first in his life, whilst on trek. He is in mid-life though has spent a fair bit of his time in Sierra Leone. However another African colleague said he had been stung as a young boy and suffered great pain for a couple of days. Another claimed to have been stung a couple of times and says applying petrol to the affected area gives relief from the pain and reduces other effects. All this reinforces my view that when you are out at night it is always worth carrying a torch so that you have some chance, though remote, of knowing what you are treading on.

On the 27th [of April 1733] at a town about a mile from Brucoe I found a monstrous large scorpion being I believe full twelve inches long ... I have known several people stung by small scorpions which give an infinite deal of pain ... records Francis Moore.

More illness:

10.05.11. I have been feeling tired and slightly sickly for the past few days and have developed a rash which I am hoping is only something like prickly heat. The rash covers my arms and hands - perhaps my back too but I can't see. It has been hot and humid and so my arms are often covered in sweat. I think the rash only covers the exposed areas of my skin but I can't be certain. Additionally my face gives a burning sensation and feels somewhat dry although I do not seem especially sunburnt. I have been checking diseases and symptoms in my guide book. A Peace Corps friend, Steph, has advised me to use 'Asepso' soap for the rash. It's always worth checking with other NGOs here if you begin to suffer from anything. You will usually find that someone has already had it and can suggest a treatment. Sometimes one catches a glimpse of why West Africa has been called 'the white man's grave' - we aren't anatomically really quite cut out for it.

Africans too have a legendary resilience to these and similar climatic conditions. One reason why they were in such demand as slaves for plantation work in the harsh conditions of the Americas was that they had at least a chance of coping with them. Indeed according to accounts I have read West Africans proved to be more able to cope with South American conditions than did the region's own indigenous peoples.

Last Sunday I invited my volunteer colleagues Sankumba and Tida around for a few snacks preceded by a glass of wine. I had managed to obtain a dubious looking bottle of white with a dried out cork and cloudy contents from a local wholesale drinks supplier. It was the best he had though I don't think he himself had any idea of what constituted a well-kept bottle of wine in good condition. As I suspected it would be, it was almost undrinkable. One does feel here that they get the worst of everything and again the claim made by the malcontent ex-pat on the coast went through my mind - 'You pay f... all and you get f... all' - although on this occasion it wasn't that cheap by local standards but nevertheless we 'got f... all'.

Before we ate I managed to induce a shocked silence when I proposed a toast to **'My Birthday'**. I hadn't told my colleagues earlier in the day that this was indeed my birthday and they weren't quite sure whether my statement was a weak attempt to be humorous. The occasion hadn't passed unmarked however receiving texts as I had from each of my three wonderful daughters as well as a skype call from them en-bloc. On this occasion the connection was thankfully good enough to conduct a meaningful conversation which didn't consist almost entirely of snatches of questions like 'Can you hear me?' And 'Can you see me?'

I am very pleased that I have managed to procure a new lavatory seat in Bansang. This may seem rather banal to report but believe you me here it is a considerable achievement. I managed to track this down in the only shop in the whole town that had one, having failed to find one in either of the thriving market towns of **Wassu** or **Brikamabah**. The shopkeeper was very reluctant to part with it separately from its accompanying ceramic pan and I had to pay over the odds to persuade him to do so.

More on marriage: I was told by a colleague recently that there are religious constraints on marrying for a man if you are unable to support a wife and potentially a family.

This may explain the generational differences in marriage partners as young men usually have not yet built up a position where they can proceed to ask for anyone's hand. Commonly here men of 40, 50 and 60 plus will marry young women in their early 20s or even younger. I think even I am regarded as having potential on this front by some!

A very large rat has been caught and killed in the next compound to our own. It seemed to have much more prominent ears than the average British rat - and to be more like images I have seen of the plague rats of old. Certainly I have heard on a number occasions about how large the bush rats here can be. Perhaps this was one. I have no doubt that this creature will find its way into a cooking pot.

18.05.15: I write with an unsteady hand as we are **on-trek to Kudang**. From the window of our four by four I can see great termite mounds like giant, extracted, rotten teeth with hairline cracks, crannies and nooks.

It is 10.30am and already the land looks too dry, arid and unyielding to support any life. But there are a few green trees and bushes scattered across the parched earth and dried out grass. The only time the landscape looks capable of supporting life is early in the morning when it holds a mist close to itself - reluctant to let the last residue of the night's moisture escape into the atmosphere above.

Now we have stopped to refuel and I can write without fear of being jolted in all directions. The petrol station is just a large patch of red earth with no shade and two petrol pumps centrally positioned. At the back of the plot is a small building with no apparent function.

The villages we pass are almost all built of wattle and mud with circular walls and conical grass roofs. As we were leaving our office breakfast was being served and our driver and the SEO on this trip have insisted on bringing some along with us so that on the seat next to me is an open bowl of oily fried onions, luncheon meat and potatoes in a sauce with a fresh loaf. If the driver has to break sharply as he often does it will go everywhere.

We are now in the last week or so of May and everyone is looking forward to the rains even with its attendant challenges just as we were looking forward to the dry season last October. **The heat has become oppressive** with a humidity that is building. Sometimes the nights are intolerable and sleeping can be all but impossible. These conditions sap ones strength and energy and to just lie in one's bed is always a temptation. Even some of my African colleagues and family find this to be so. Additionally there have been problems with the power supply recently so that sometimes we have to endure the whole evening without light or fans. There is no schedule for this so that the supply is unpredictable. For lighting during such periods we try to survive on candles during the hours of darkness. There are two wind-up lamps but they tend not to last long so that one is forever winding them up. We do have battery powered lamps too which are not always very efficient and the batteries are not always easily procurable.

The rains will cool everything down but bring with them hordes of insects and even greater humidity levels. Western residents here who have the choice will often desert the region altogether during the wet season and hotels will close.

Moore writes:

> ... *Four months in the year are unhealthy and very tedious to those who are come out of a colder climate; but the perpetual spring, where you commonly see ripe fruit and blossoms on the same tree make some amends for that inconvenience. The air is very pleasant and refreshing but it has something so very peculiar that the keys in your pocket will rust.*

I would call it humidity!

The longer I stay here the harder it gets. When I think about what I miss most about life back home many of these things are really very basic and no doubt unexciting to anyone who has them on demand. I miss being able to have a proper haircut – a Western haircut instead of choosing between a shaved head or amateurishly chiselled hair. I miss light in the evenings after dark [as I write we have had no power for 6 nights – I light a single candle usually so that I don't get through my supply of them too quickly or increase the temperature unduly]. I miss being cooler and not having my shirt stuck to my back with sweat. I miss having a choice of food – food which is not rice, bread or groundnuts. I dare not think of cheese. I miss having a comfortable chair to sit on or sofa to lie on or a cool room in which to snooze when my energy has been completely sapped by the heat. I miss a clean bathroom with no bugs, especially with no cockroaches, that drains properly and where the shower drain doesn't gurgle, bubble and often fill up when you flush the loo. I miss a bathroom where you can't hear things running around in the roof space just above your head not knowing what is doing the running. I miss my short walks into the centre of the London 'village' where I live for a leisurely breakfast or perhaps to grab a designer coffee with my daughters for half an hour or so before they catch the tube to work or college etc. I miss a good newspaper, friends of my own age and outlook and indeed on this front have had to develop reserves of self-reliance of which even Emerson would have been proud.

I miss English beer, pubs and restaurants. I don't miss television. I miss not having to worry about what insects are crawling across my floor. I miss regular access to the internet with a connection speed that doesn't drive you insane. I miss driving my car. I miss football and cricket or regular reports of them. I feel deprived of almost everything I value except my notebook and one crucially important thing that makes life here possible - the proximity not of friends but of decent and caring human beings with whom I share my home and my life, though not my culture, because my *kunda* folk, my African family, are pure gold.

The kora is a most distinctive Mandinka instrument the sound of which evokes the West African landscape and the rhythm of life of its peoples. It usually has twenty-one strings and a sound box made from a large gourd. Traditionally it will often be played as a solo instrument and the player will sing along. There is a great deal of repetition and the words are very important. They will often carry a moral teaching or even promote the President [can't imagine that happening in the UK but then we don't have a 'big man' culture and dissent is tolerated]. The sentiments and the emotions are often understated and one might say 'laid back' such as is the case with a traditionalist like Amadu Bansang Jobarteh or even the more commercialised Jaliba Kuyateh who has amplified his voice and kora and combines them with percussion and other instruments.

There are five principal Mandinka **griot families** in The Gambia that is to say families which pass on from one generation to the next the knowledge and skills of storytelling, musical performance, poetic recitation and oral history – indeed they constitute the troubadour tradition of this place. Other exponents of the kora include Lamin Saho, Papa Susso, Foday Musa Suso and most recently Sona Jobarteh of mixed Gambian and British parentage and unusually and perhaps uniquely, a female exponent.

I spotted **a monitor lizard** today, about three feet long, walking along our compound wall and then climbing the tree opposite my door at the near end of our vegetable plot within the compound yard. I made the mistake of telling our compound children who immediately raised the alarm with a cry of 'Snake, snake!' as all they could see at first glance was its long tail wrapped around an upper branch. In no time every child in the immediate vicinity came through the compound gate with sticks, clubs, stones and rocks prepared to beat the creature to death. One of our own older children, Mohamed, shook and poked the lizard out of the tree whilst the dozen or so children stood by ready with their killing implements in hands. I intervened to prevent this, scolded them and explained that the animal was completely harmless. Eventually they dispersed and the animal found shelter under a pile of building blocks in the yard.

Bush Meat:This creature we spotted several times over the next few days and weeks within the compound and it was all I could do to prevent its being killed. Our girls, who were frightened of it, would throw bricks at it whenever it appeared. I explained again that it was harmless [having double checked this with my guide book just to be sure] and I said that it was probably doing us the useful service of living off the cockroaches that live in and around our latrines. Upon my return from the UK where I spent some weeks over the forthcoming school summer closure period, I noticed that somehow this creature was still present and had survived without my protection though our girls continued to aim bricks at it whenever it appeared. A work colleague told me that these creatures are perfectly edible although some sub species more so than others. He didn't care for the banded variety apparently.

Moore reports:

> *Here are also plenty of Guanas ... a very ugly creature which resembles a little alligator ... The natives and some white men eat this for a dainty bit; and I am told they eat as well as any rabbit.*

In my experience most Africans where I lived would eat most bush meat when they could get it. On one occasion whilst I was chatting casually to one of our SEOs, **Biram Faye**, sitting outside on a veranda at the regional directorate office I saw a squirrel and happened to mention to him that that was the first one I'd seen since I'd been there. '**What squirrel?**' said Biram. 'That one', I said pointing it out to him. No sooner had Biram located the creature visually than he was up on his feet and in full pursuit, picking up rocks to hurl as it as he went. It was with some relief to me that he returned empty handed, the squirrel having just managed to escape over our perimeter wall. When I asked why he had taken against the creature he said that he just wanted to eat it. He subsequently explained that he had managed to catch two pigeons the night before by dazzling them with a torch whilst they roosted on a low branch on one of our Directorate compound trees. Biram lived on site and had been disturbed from sleep by their cooing. Apparently the birds were cooked and eaten with immediate effect and Biram had gone back to bed.

I remember too that a volunteer colleague based on the north bank at Kerewan reported that she had eaten a dish made by her African family/neighbours from a **hyena** that had been shot close by – indeed we were shown photographs of the animal before it was cooked in evidence.

My own **bush meat** experience I think I mentioned earlier which was bush pig – dry and gamy but very tasty served one evening during a visit to the safari camp across the river from my settlement.

Moore says:

> ... There is scarce anything which they [the natives] do not eat; large snakes, guanas, monkeys, pelicans, bald eagles, alligators and sea-horses ...

Belief in Magic, Superstition and the Marabout Tradition

> Our compound leader Faa Bakari has recently attended the funeral of his niece. He tells me that she had never been well since giving birth to her last baby just five months ago. Faa Bakari was unable to tell me what was the precise problem but he says that the doctors who had been treating her had

advised her to seek the assistance of a marabout. Were they saying that as far as they were concerned they had done all that could be done through conventional medicine? I don't know but this story underlines once more the strength of the local belief in magic and superstition and the continuing acceptance of an animist approach. The marabout tradition integrates traditional magic with Islamic beliefs.

One encounters always and everywhere the wearing of charms, *safo*, for protection and good luck and sometimes verses from the Koran are written out and placed in a pouch tied somewhere about an individual.

Further it is quite common for illnesses or accidents to be put down to the bad intentions of someone who wishes the victim harm; to the casting of a spell.

The other day some visitors to my compound, young women probably in their twenties, came to see friends who brought them to say hello to me. These young women were explaining that the original Sariang - the town's second Imam, Sariang Jabbeh, the one after whom I am named indirectly through Faa Bakari's father, could remove the crown of his head like a cap and set it down on the table and could then replace it. They were firmly convinced that that this is a true story. I asked why he would do this but received no clear answer.

Another example: A colleague at my office, a senior education officer, explained that there are relatively few Gambian war dead buried in the war graves cemetery in Fajara because people here have secret potions and other ways that can prevent bullets etc. from passing through their bodies.

Moore says:

> ... when the Mandingoes [Mandinka] are going into battle they put so much faith in these Mohammedans as to go and buy papers of them so charmed as they believe to prevent the person who wears it from being shot ... and they pay for [someone who] ... encloses it in leather ... and they wear them across their shoulders ...

This practice remains alive and well.

> My colleague also claims to have a relative who can brush the leaves of some trees which then turn into money and flutter down to the ground - he claims to have seen his relative do this.
>
> Again there are the quite commonly instances of proclaimed devil possession, instances of 'falling down', that I have already noted. Almost every Gambian I have spoken to accepts that these cases are authentic.
>
> At one point I asked around my town about the fabled river monster I had read about in the guide books - sometimes called '**Ninki Nanka**'. Of the half dozen people I asked on separate occasions none disputed its existence and four claimed to have seen it for themselves - including my landlord Faa Bakari. When I asked what it looked like he said '... a bit like a man'. I considered carefully whether these responses might just be made up to give the *toubab* the answer they thought he wanted but I was convinced that they were sincere. I don't believe that my landlord especially is at all into that game - by now we know each other well as members of the same family.'

No scientific evidence has ever been established to confirm the existence of this mythic creature.

Moore tells us that:

> *... as I was walking about a quarter of a mile from Joar factory I found the foot of a beast, the carcass having been devoured, as I believe by a lion, much resembling a baboon but as big as that of a man, it was newly killed, covered in hair about an inch long ... the natives they told us that it was the foot of what they called a Wild Man, that there are a good many of them in this country but they are seldom found; they are as tall as a man, have breasts like a woman and have a sort of a language and walk upon their feet as human creatures.*

On one occasion I heard in the bedroom next to mine in our compound, what I took to be someone having a conversation on a phone

– rather inconsiderately I felt as it commenced in the small hours of the morning and then continued for an inordinately long time – for at least two and maybe as much as three hours. I did not complain immediately and tried to get what sleep I could. In the morning however I felt I should say something to someone about it but when I mentioned the occurrence I was told that it was a marabout – he was chanting and reciting various things as he went through a ritual.

I wondered in relation to this ritual, what was it meant to achieve and what/who was meant to be the object of it. It has occurred to me since that the answer to this latter question might have been me – lying in my bed throughout the whole process just a few inches away on the other side of the wall having 'stubbornly' failed, as others might see it, to ask for the hand of any of the unmarried daughters of the compound. Perhaps this was meant to put me in mind to choose one.

> There is here a deeply held commitment to gnostic belief, to the professed tribal mysteries, knowledge of which allows an individual to begin their transition to adulthood such as those passed on during the Mandinka Kankurang festival. We can only speculate about these mysteries for an outsider can have no access to them. They must never be divulged.

Palm Wine, Cooking and More Insects

> Although the wet season has commenced we are relatively bug-free perhaps because it has really only rained heavily once about five or six days ago. Even so – as usual apparently – the morning after this first rain we had what looked like **flying termites** - clouds of them. On two evenings I have had flying ants until 9pm in my house, attracted by the light. Tonight a gecko joined me in my bedroom and a **large, flat, very black spider.** Also I intercepted and squashed a cockroach in my sitting room/kitchen and just avoided locking in **a praying mantis** with me tonight in my house as I bolted my outside door. I know this is only the start of the insect invasion. My experience starting last August has taught me

what to expect. I hope I can endure it because it makes me feel very uneasy.

The women here cook on open wood fires in **cauldrons** (*kaleeroo*) of all sizes. The rice, nuts and millet etc. will often have to be pounded first in a large, **wooden pestle** (*kuluno*) with a heavy **four or five foot mortar** (*kudaa*). The women have to be very strong to do the pounding. Having tried my hand at it I found I tired very quickly.

There are large slotted utensils to stir, drain and turn over the food whilst cooking. Much of the meat and much else, is deep fried here – for example an omelette is deep fried. Prodigious amounts of palm oil are used.

We tried the local **palm wine** (*tenjiyo*) recently. Everyone tells you it is best drunk fresh, i.e. the same day it's made. The sample we had was watery and cloudy white – a bit like lemon juice to look at and vaguely similar to taste but not as sharp. It had a very unpleasant smell – but the taste is much more tolerable. In terms of its body the liquid was very light. We were told that if you keep it longer it gets stronger but also the smell is even worse. We were told that of the palm species occurring locally they tend to tap the oil and raffia palms but not the coconut palms.

Apparently until quite recently there were three compounds producing palm wine in our town – all Christian families – but now this has reduced to one as two of them have converted to Islam. As everywhere there is a propensity to gravitate towards the norm.

The palm tapping tradition is said to flourish amongst the Manjagos, a sub set of the Jolas, who are usually Christian but occasionally Animist.

Moore writes:
> ... *And here perhaps it is not improper to mention the palm tree ... out of it the natives extract a sort of white liquor like whey called palm wine by making an incision at the top of the tree to which they apply gourd bottles; into them runs the liquor by means of a pipe which they make of leaves.*

This wine is very pleasant to drink as soon as drawn, being extraordinarily sweet, but is apt to purge very much. In a day or two it ferments, grows hard and strong, like Rhenish wine, at which time the natives drink it in abundance.

On Trek in the footsteps of Mungo Park

Today we went east along a deeply rutted dirt road on the north bank. It ran from just outside the ferry point across the river at Lamin Koto. We travelled almost to the point on the river from which Mungo Park commenced both his famed journeys upstream into the interior in 1795 and 1805 but not quite because no road goes all the way there. We were anyway bound for the closest extant settlement - in Park's day it was called **Pisania** and was a British trading post. Park spent about six months here before his first trip studying the Mandinka language as the guest of a surgeon called Dr John Laidley. His objective was to trace the course of the Niger. The settlement today is named **Karantaba**. Of the Pisania Park knew and the trading post itself as far as I know nothing visible now remains. Closer to the river is a decaying monument to Park at the point from which he is thought to have embarked. To reach it requires local knowledge. The contemporary settlement of Karantaba is wattle-fenced, dirt-roaded and mud-bespattered. It looks as if it is part of and grows out of the very earth it occupies.

We had come to heal a dispute between the head teacher and his deputy at the local secondary school. One maintained that the other had been using one of the precious pupil bicycles, procured by special funding, to get himself to work - the other that of course he had - wasn't it important after all that the staff were there to teach the pupils. Journeys to school here are often long and by foot can be almost impractical but may be made possible by a bicycle.

The vengeance in the air was tangible. Our Principle Education Officer, using that phrase I had heard before, implored both parties to the dispute to 'Remember that you are

The Mungo Park memorial near Karantaba close to the point where he embarked on his trip up the Gambia River

Muslims'. As a mere non-Muslim I tried to point out that their primary focus needed to be the children and their needs and how they could best be met. I wondered how they thought their dispute assisted them in serving that objective. Eventually we extracted a commitment from them to do their best to work together. We left hoping that matters had moved forward but with no firm belief that they had.

The Deep Shame of Having a Boyfriend, Approaches to Wife Procurement and Polygamy

I had a conversation at work today with several of my male Gambian colleagues throwing into sharp relief a cultural difference between my host and my own native cultures. I happened to refer to '... my daughter's boyfriend ...' This solicited great shock and pity on the part of my colleagues, many of them fathers. They were so sorry for me that any father should feel they had to admit and especially so publicly, the shame that a daughter of his had a boyfriend. Here for a girl or young woman to have a boyfriend is regarded as an irreparable moral lapse which impugns her virginity and makes marriage all but impossible. When I tried to explain my own culture's norms there seemed to be no ability on my colleagues' part to comprehend that having a boyfriend is commonly a prelude to marriage and indeed usually an essential prerequisite for there to be a marriage at all.

Invariably whenever my volunteer female colleagues had their boyfriends coming out to visit and stay with them they would introduce them to their African hosts as their husband for fear that their reputation would suffer badly and perhaps make their position difficult or even untenable.

One further indication of the way things worked differently in The Gambia is illustrated by the following. Whilst being visited by my daughters from the UK I received a phone call from an unknown male who gave me a brief prospectus of himself – he was a lawyer he said. He then asked my permission to speak to one of my daughters on the phone there and then although he had never met any of us. His sister, a friend/acquaintance of one of my compound girls, both of whom were with us at the time had phoned him just a moment before. The sister knew her brother was looking for another wife. On the basis of this sister's description he had decided that one of my daughters might fit the bill and got my phone number from our compound girl and phoned me without delay. At times like this the cultural divide is so great that one is lost for words in trying to explain why such a request is inappropriate.

> An *ustaz* [koranic teacher] said to me today, when someone raised the issue of **female circumcision**, though not an Islamic requirement it is supported as a guideline by the Hadith. It helps to prevent women from looking outside their marriage [presumably for sexual gratification]. He also said polygamy is the right solution for men as they are always ready for sex and having a number of wives helps to meet this need. I couldn't help but feel he was confirming some of the worst suspicions relating to the practice held by many of its critics in the West.

Once More to the Coast

> 26.06.2011 I am back in the Kombos on NGO business once more, specifically in Fajara and the rains have truly returned for another season. We had a downpour at about lunchtime here today. It is now 9.30pm in the evening and there are flying termites everywhere and microscopic ants - also some very small lizards. Before the wet season is over they will be big and fat.
>
> Last night here in my hotel there seemed to be **more mosquitos than even in Janjanbureh** and this morning when I woke I found a trail of bites running along my right arm - which is the one I use to prop up my head when I rest and sleep and which therefore sticks out from under my sheet.

Moore writes:

> *... I lay all night at the house of the Alcade ... on a matt raised with small forked sticks and having nothing over me*

to keep the mosquitoes from me I was miserably bit by them and got very little rest.

These mosquitoes are the greatest plague to one's person of any other vermin on the river ...

I must be up at 5.30am tomorrow so as to catch the 7pm Bara ferry. From the ferry point on the other side of the river estuary we will travel by sept-place. I will be travelling with a Peace Corps friend, Steph, and VSO colleague Tida. This evening I will just be able to fit in a draft Julbrew in the bar downstairs before taking a taxi to Senegambia to meet my friend **TJ** at a Moroccan restaurant. He is still full of ideas discussed previously of our investing in a currently failing hotel/restaurant at Turntable. He has already spoken to the freeholder about rent and has identified a UK trained, ambitious young Gambian manager who could run it for us who is presently employed just a short distance from it in a failing restaurant. He thinks all we need is £20,000 to get the restaurant started. The forty-four room hotel part of the premises TJ thinks could become operational later once the restaurant is properly established. Sounds as if he sees my role as simply providing/raising the capital needed and to watch the investment grow exponentially from a distance in the UK - Don't think so!

Back to Janjanbureh

More carping ex-pats! As I have noted previously one comes across European ex-pat residents and regular visitors here who have nothing good to say about the country or its people. We have currently in our town a British couple who fit this description. They have retired and travel a lot. They have bought a piece of land down by the river's edge and right in the centre of our town. They want to develop it as a tourist facility. They have had the plot for a while but move forward incrementally on this project - doing construction work as and when they can afford to do so. They are here very infrequently and have owned the land for some time.

> The land is fertile and as I say on the bank of the river, so that when they are away local people come and plant vegetables on the part of the plot nearest the river. They are thinking why waste unused land and are attracted by the fact that they don't have to walk far to get their watering done. It's the casual way things work here.

[Moore writes:
> *... In these countries the natives are not avaricious of lands; they desire no more than what they use ...'*

Ownership here is not always seen in quite the same as we see it back home. An African in a village not far from my settlement whose family were all either dead or dispersed elsewhere was told by the village chief that if she doesn't occupy her family compound, though it has been in her family for many generations, he would allocate it to someone else.

> The couple are angry about the temporary residence of the gardeners, although they are not building anything on the land right next to the river where the gardens have sprung up but rather at the back of the plot. But they complain about everything and talk about how the people in this country are only interested in taking money from Westerners [there are frequent requests for money especially if they think you are a tourist but they have very little], how everything has been provided by this or that NGO such as school buildings, state vehicles, health establishments etc. [it's called helping people less well off than yourself though efficient use of donated resources is sometimes wanting!], how the Africans never run anything properly [sometimes I feel a little sympathy with this], how poor are their standards of hygiene [my compound family almost always shower and change their clothes twice a day not counting ritual washing for prayers, although one frequently sees goats etc. eating out of the compound's food bowls in unguarded moments: bowls which then receive a cold water rinse only often without the assistance of any form of soap]. These same people

seem heartily sick of the place and one wonders why on earth they remain even though they don't have to stay here or visit. When I am exposed to this sort of carping I think to myself that I hope I don't get like that or that I leave before I do.

This couple also number amongst another sub-category of residents/frequent visitor *toubabs* namely **those who think they are immune to malaria** and therefore don't take anti-malarial medication regularly. You come across them not infrequently. They say 'I don't catch malaria!' There is one of these buried somewhere in the grounds of his own safari camp which lies on the road from our township to the island's western tip. I heard the sorry tale of his passing from another expat who knew him well. He had lived here for several years apparently - but you really don't want to find out whether you are right in believing you have a natural immunity to malaria by catching for example cerebral malaria because it is fatal with some regularity.

Of course if you live here permanently or for more than two years you will face a dilemma anyway because the medical advice is that you can't stay on this medication indefinitely without serious risk to your health.

I have started to throw stones at the cats that come into our compound from the one next door - just like the girls in our compound do. One will often wake to find that a cat has reduced a batch of new chicks from half a dozen to nothing overnight. With the kind of domestic arrangements people have here with much roaming and vulnerable livestock that are such an important food source, I think it's really anti-social to keep such things as cats.

The Volunteer Community:

The volunteer community in this country is of some size. Although there are probably only about thirty or so **VSO** volunteers there are several other organisations represented here. The biggest group as far as I can tell is the **American Peace Corps** which numbers around a hundred. In the vicinity of my township, Janjanbureh, we have maybe twelve to fifteen Peace Corps volunteers. With the exception of one recent arrival, Joanna, they don't live in town but singly in the surrounding villages and have no regular access to a power supply. Because of their situation, learning and speaking the most prevalent local tribal language is essential and their organisation keeps a careful watch on their progress in the acquisition of this both prior to and during their placement. Usually they live in traditional housing - wattle and daube huts with grass roofs and are mostly young and not long out of college. I am always impressed at how well they bear the difficult conditions here especially as they have to sign up for a stint of duty of over two years which at their age must seem interminable. I like their generally open and outgoing nature. They seem so free of the circumspection and initial suspicion I meet so often amongst my own countrymen and women.

In addition to the Americans we have **Swedes** [e.g. FIOH Future in Our Hands] and other Scandinavians. Then **Horse and Donkey** - a British charity which works to improve the treatment of those animals and does other work [for example a couple of its people bummed a lift in one of our Regional Education vehicles during one of our school visit trips so they could install some fly screens in the classrooms at one school.

There is a natural inclination to bond within the volunteer community as fellow *toubabs* away from home with challenges in common and on a similar mission.

On Work Duty

I attended the **scholarship competition/pageant** this Saturday night. This is a national competition with regional heats to select a senior secondary girl who will be financed to go through university in The Gambia [there is only one].

Worryingly the criteria by which candidates are judged include standard of costume/dress, performance talent, beauty and poise - but no mention of academic achievement.

I attended as a representative of the Regional Education Directorate and was asked to chair the panel of judges for the Central River Region heat. I and another NGO education office judge marked the girls with all the same scores, in fact full marks, for the more onerous criteria so as to reduce the effect of these as much as possible as significant factors in the outcome of the competition. However I don't think our fellow judge from and representing our local prison service did the same.

Typically the event which was scheduled for 9pm didn't start until 11pm but on this occasion there was a good reason, namely, particularly heavy rains and **thunderstorms**. In fact only half the candidates and schools were able to get to the event, six schools instead of twelve. We didn't complete presentations and deliberations until well into the early hours.

I remember whilst waiting for contestants and their supporters to arrive having a conversation with an African colleague about why thunderstorms in this part of the world are so much feared. I was prompted to do this when I noticed real fear in many attendees around me as the storm broke overhead. It conjured a memory of my grandmother back home, when I was little, sitting in the cupboard under the stairs terrified whenever we had a thunderstorm and I noted in my own mind that this fear there, back home, seemed now to have gone for most of us. I wondered whether the fear here was tied up with their basic animist beliefs. My colleague made no reference to these but said that, unlike in the West where he understood we knew how to manage thunder and lightning, here they did not and that not uncommonly people were struck by lightning. As if to confirm his position and that the fear around me had been well founded I made an entry the following day in my journal based on circumstances that we learnt had come to pass:

We heard that in a rice field near a village just across the river from our island and just south of our position a married couple were struck by lightning and the man fatally so.

... Both thunder and lightning are very dreadful, the one flashing so quick makes it continually light and the other shakes the very ground under you ...

writes Moore

One of the Director's ewes was **found dead** yesterday morning on the veranda at a doorway outside the office in which I am based at the Directorate. A small flock of his sheep grazes in the grounds of our offices and apparently this is the third sheep he has lost recently. Most of my colleagues are of the opinion that the deaths are due to snake bite. I was struck how the other flock members would not leave the dead ewe alone and occasionally nuzzled it as if trying to push it to its feet. When eventually one of our gardeners came to remove the carcass unceremoniously in a wheelbarrow which the other sheep witnessed, they remained where she had died and even sporadically tried to push their way into our office door as if they thought she might be within.

A noteworthy item was raised by our PEO at a Directorate meeting held this Saturday with our cluster monitors who each have under their care a local subset of the schools within the Directorate's region. He requested that they behave more professionally towards female staff when visiting schools. Some female teachers had complained about the attentions paid to them by some of their cluster monitors. The guidance given on this at the meeting was **'Leave the female staff alone unless you intend to marry them'**. There were titters all round except from the PEO who dealt with the matter with due formality. I wondered how much more seriously this issue would have to be taken by all concerned in the environment from which I had come. I wondered too how one was meant to determine whether one wanted to marry a particular female school employee without first paying some attention to her and getting to know her and establishing whether she was willing. But then I remembered the poster campaign that one frequently encountered in our schools which entreated all who needed reminding 'Before you marry her ask her!'

Annual Presidential Visit: 'Dialogue with the People'

Today I travelled from Janjanbureh west along the North Bank Road in one of our Directorate vehicles to **Kaur** with the PEO and a couple of SEOs.

Moore:
> *... Cower [Kaur], where is the greatest resort of people and the most trade of any town in the whole river, for it is to this place that the merchants always bring their slaves provided that they are not in a great haste to return home and cannot meet with a good market for them before they come down so low ...*

Our mission was to inspect arrangements along this route for the President's visit to our region. This annual up-country trip is promoted as the President's 'Dialogue with the People' tour.

We spent some of the morning and afterwards most of the afternoon giving support and advice to the teachers who were looking after their pupils in clumps along the route. Our object was to maximise child safety and, apparently, to ensure the appropriateness of banners! The presidential convoy would be sweeping in from the next adjacent region to our west along the road from the capital and the coast.

I asked my Directorate colleagues whether the visit was an official state visit or a party visit. I was told the former. In that case I asked 'Why were the President's party flags and garb so prevalent en route in the villages instead of the national flag?' I was told that the question was indiscreet and that I could trust no one - that anyone might inform a relevant agency about such an inappropriate question.

At Kaur, his first stop in our region has been scheduled and through the baking afternoon a very large crowd, marshalled sometimes quite roughly by police and troops, gathered expectantly and excitedly around a large, open, dirt expanse in the middle of the town. As time went on rumours began circulating with growing frequency of the Big Man's imminent arrival. He did so at last in the very late afternoon and with much ceremony. The loudspeaker system that had been broadcasting music for much of the waiting period was now turned up to full blast and through an entrance formed by a gap in the crowds created by a police cordon there came in the African manner a stream of **out-runners** gyrating manically – many scores of them in fact perhaps a hundred or more. Eventually at their rear the presidential Hummer came into view. The runners formed a ringed bodyguard around the President whilst he stood at the back of the vehicle as it moved forward and waved his Koran in response to the crowds. Their apparent adulation expressed itself in frenzied cheering and the performance of a traditional greeting/salute gesture consisting of outstretched arms and hands waving up and down rapidly from the wrists only with fingers spread towards the object of their adulation. In some cases this was no doubt spontaneous and sincere – in others it would simply have been expedient.

The President was dressed in his familiar brilliant white African robes and white pillbox hat which gave him a truly messianic appearance. One could see how easily anyone might be swept up by the whole occasion to pledge their unconditional loyalty and service to **the Big Man**. A voice in the back of my head however repeated the injunction – 'There is no God but God'.

After a number of circumnavigations of the 'arena' the presidential vehicle halted and he alighted to seat himself in the largest and most comfortable looking chair at the midpoint of a line of chairs at one long side of the arena facing the crowd at its thickest point opposite whilst it calmed itself a little.

There followed a procession of speakers that addressed the audience through a PA system. One by one they extolled the virtues and achievements of the President.

Although I was not able to stay any longer I was told that the great man himself would be speaking at this event towards the end of the proceedings. It was a release not to have to stay any longer as contributions became increasingly tedious.

Our directorate party left in our vehicle to do a last check of the groups of school children who had been waiting all day along the remainder of the presidential convoy's route from Kaur to Janjanbureh. Many had walked from their schools and villages through tracks in the bush to the North Bank Road, often to a desolate spot, so as to be in place by early morning in case there was an earlier than scheduled appearance of the President. They had been waiting through the heat of the day, marshalled by their teachers, armed with branches they had plucked from the trees and some banners to wave at the President as he passed. Mostly these groupings of children had inadequate food and water provisions and no latrine facilities. Now, well into the evening and as the light faded, their long vigil was not yet over but even so they managed an enthusiastic reception for ourselves as we passed. It was sad to contemplate that most of them would catch not even a blurred glimpse of the President as he sped past in his convey in the darkness - a convoy that invariably travelled at high speed as if every section of the route presented opportunity for his political opponents to mount a serious challenge to his person and position.

At last we arrived back at the ferry-point at Lamin Koto to catch the ferry across the river to Janjanbureh and as we crossed I could see that a great crowd had gathered at the terminal on the far bank, behind an army cordon, in anticipation of the President's arrival which had been scheduled for 11pm. In the event he did not arrive until well after midnight by which time I myself was embedded in the throng with a number of NGO colleagues and acquaintances. As the President disembarked in his Hummer to take the salutations of the crowd packets of biscuits flew out in all directions from his vehicle causing a great surge which seemed to come from those at the back. We all lurched forward dangerously so and many, including myself, were unable to keep their footing. I landed sans my expensive Canadian bush-hat in a crush and unholy pile on top of a young Peace Corps friend of mine, Katie from Virginia. Given the loss of personal space I was pleased it was her rather than anyone else and glad too that no one was seriously hurt. I was only reunited with my hat after greasing the palm of a local African boy who had it in his keeping and who I suspect had been watching my increasingly frantic searches for it for some time. In all probability a replacement would not have been procurable anywhere in the length and breadth of the country.

It is now mid-July and the cauldron days of March to early June have now given way to the sticky days of the wet season. Fans remain necessary almost every day and evening. The full onslaught of the rains and insects is now imminent.

However I leave for a 7 week break in the UK this Sunday which in all honesty I need badly.

Out of Africa

In response to the deprivations of my African situation, back in London I gorged myself on theatre and cinema visits, pubs, restaurants, sessions of talk and drink with friends, shopping trips for essential items and gifts for my return and much else for seven weeks during which time a second ingrowing toenail was also attended to. As the toe was not infected this time the whole process was much less painful than before and following treatment I was able to return to my African home for the last time to undertake the final few months of my service.

Return to Africa

10.09.2011. I am back in Africa to find that our NGO's **new batch of volunteers** arrived a week ago. Cultural differences between what they know and what they will find here are often unsurprisingly either disbelieved by them or put down to the naivety of Africans and to much else when reported to them by more seasoned volunteers. There is no sense yet on the part of most of the new recruits to whom I have spoken that their own way of seeing the world is largely a contingency learnt/acquired/absorbed along with its values. There is no understanding yet that this way of seeing could have been different nor that there is no absolute and independent reference point from which they can compare what they know and see with what their hosts here know and see. This patronising and culturally arrogant position is of course hard to avoid because we have no other way to process or interpret new experiences/perceptions. But realising this last truth is what takes time and once understood, if it is understood well, our humility in the face of difference will emerge and be more correctly proportionate. We must always beware of our tendency to **cultural imperialism** coming from the so-called Developed World and remember that not everything we come across requires a judgement on our part - moral or otherwise.

11.09.2011. Saw my first warthogs today, known here as **bush pigs**. They suddenly broke cover and dashed across the North Bank Road just in front of our directorate four wheel drive as we returned from on-trek to a local school. There was a family of three of them. They looked strong, healthy and muscular and were led by a fierce male with formidable tusks which exited his muzzle laterally and then curved upwards and round ultimately terminating at the top of his snout. They looked much bigger than I expected they would – about the size of an adult domesticated pig unless my memory has exaggerated this.

Just an amusing little incident perhaps worthy of note: having bought myself a new camera whilst back in the U.K. I was able to donate my old one to my African compound family last night. I gave it to Faa Bakari but asked that its use be shared by all. They all looked very pleased with it but tonight one young boy, perhaps nine or ten years old startled me by knocking on my fly screen door and calling my name from the darkness outside. When I drew back the door curtain he looked straight at me through the screen and said **'Sariang, next time you go to America you bring me bike please'**.

Termites:

I have just noticed a recurrence of the termite problem with my table. All the furniture here is VSO standard issue and made of cheap plywood which of course by local standards is good – many people here have little or no furniture at all. This is the second time I have noted termites in my table with the tell-tale piles of very fine sawdust beneath it. Last time I applied my insect spray to the infected area trying to penetrate as many holes with it as possible but without any real hope it would work. No doubt if one scoured the Kombos back on the coast for the right insecticide treatment one might find it but up-country here one would be very lucky to come across such a thing I am sure.

Moore experienced something similar, he writes:

> ... I was not more afraid of their [the Company's goods] being stole than of being spoiled by pernicious vermin called buggabuggs; they are very destructive wherever they get ... they are a sort of white ant ... they feed as heartily upon wood as anything at all ... they eat the inside only of a chest or table so that when they have entirely destroyed it by eating the heart and substance of the wood yet do they appear to the eye to be still sound ...

Climate and Power Supply: am not sure I could ever describe even the early mornings here as 'crisp' although certainly during the dry season everything is brittle through sheer lack of moisture and dust reigns supreme everywhere.

But this is a land of extremes and in the wet season there is no time when there is not moisture in the air – even in the cooler small hours there is the warmth and the wetness. It is as if you are living in an incubator where all that is slimy, slithering, nascent and new can thrive and proliferate to one's own discomfort. Perhaps the primal soup at the beginning of time where life first evolved '... in the first spinning place ...'[1] was just like this.

26.09.2011: there is no electricity so far this evening. The power should have come on almost an hour ago. Also the meeting that was scheduled to start at 4pm when the Regional Director returned from the Kombos did not start as he hasn't arrived. The Cluster Monitors have almost all turned up at the Directorate Office from across the region and are awaiting his appearance but it's now 8pm and there's still no sign of him. I have given up and come home to sit in the dark. I got here on my motorbike with no headlight as it's recently ceased to function and I have already contacted our support organisation to try to get it fixed. But there is always a delay in getting anything done. I have avoided the need to cook this evening as I grabbed a coffee and a roast corn cob at the small shack café at the ferry point on my way home. This

---

[1] words by Dylan Thomas, *Fern Hill*

will mean I won't be adding to the temperature levels in my small house more than necessary. It's very humid with no fans operating and there are a lot of insects on the wing tonight. I have sustained several bites to my ankles and feet generally already. I now intend to fill the remainder of my evening, with the assistance of my head-torch, by reading - I am well into Ayn Rand's *The Fountainhead* presently. In some of her descriptive passages she writes as if she's trying to create an expressionist painting. I hope that the head torch does not make my face a target for anything flying in my living room.

More about Work

As it is early in the new school year the Directorate has been carrying out a number of school visits to see how this year's revised allocation of staff and resources has settled down. We have come across several teacher shortages and many battles continue to be fought by head teachers for more staff, changes of staff, additional resources and so on. Sometimes a school will not know which of the staff allocated are actually going to turn up for the new year until it commences. Today we visited a school where the head had been sleeping on his office floor for a number of weeks, as there seems to be no appropriate accommodation in the local village. Many local compounds will not accept male tenants to live amongst them and their womenfolk.

In October 2011 for a variety of reasons, including the realisation that our Regional Director was determined to resist any real and meaningful input from me in terms of the broad issues – and following a minor disagreement with a volunteer colleague locally that got blown up out of all reasonable proportion by an inept in-country HQ and the unhelpful intervention of a meddlesome volunteer colleague based in Banjul – but also with the general feeling that my time here was up and my tolerance for the conditions spent, **I gave notice to my NGO that I was resigning my position.** I did this with a view to leaving my placement and being back home in London for Christmas.

By now I had outlasted both the other Education Management Reginal Directorate Advisors in the country in other regions by some distance – we three having arrived in the same volunteer cohort. The interim period before my departure gave opportunity to tie up any Directorate tasks/projects still unfinished and to take on any additional ones that could be accommodated.

Madrassas: As the wet season came to an end and our Directorate was able once more to pursue a more intensive series of treks to our schools, one thing I focussed on was to help step up a programme of visits to the madrassas that fell under our auspices, and indeed to a couple that did not but which aspired so to do. There was a system by which once an institution had reached a certain standard by itself, it might then qualify for adoption and some support by the Region.

One thing we wanted to know more about was progress, methods and standards in the delivery of English. Its delivery in these institutions carried a greater burden in achieving success because mostly the curriculum was delivered in Arabic. A further objective was to take stock of resource needs. By using my motorcycle for many of the visits we avoided having to compete with other directorate projects/tasks that required the use of our directorate four-wheel drive vehicles and their finite petrol allowances. This survey was led by one of our two Directorate *Oustas* [Koranic

The author on trek with Ahmed an *oustas*,
one of two at our directorate

teachers] namely, Ahmed. The two of them were responsible for co-ordinating madrassas across the Region.

Our first visit was to a **small unadopted madrassa just east of Bansang** on the South Bank Road that led ultimately to Basse. Picture a low bench no more than a foot high, bone dry and grey as if a primitive relic from a bygone age, its seating capacity extended at each end by a line of upturned, re-cycled, gallon paint tins and various other containers. This represented the seating facilities in the first classroom I entered. The window openings, both of them, no longer contained any frames, if indeed they ever did and were now larger than originally built and irregular in shape forming apertures big enough to walk through to gain access to the plot of ground behind the school building. At the head of the room, in the usual manner one came across commonly within our schools, was a large, shiny, rectangular patch of black paint on the wall. This was the blackboard. It had written upon it neatly today's Koranic verse, there to be learnt by heart. The small storeroom next door contained the madrassa's meagre resources including a small supply of chalk and a few books but no class sets of text books and little else. On the other side of this small room was another classroom only marginally better equipped than the first with a few desks and intended for the older children. Children would not be allowed to progress from one to the other however until they had reached a particular standard which sometimes led to very large boys and girls remaining with the new entrants and younger children. There were no latrine facilities I was told and pupils had to use the plot of ground behind this building to both relieve themselves and to use as a playground area. The sole remaining teacher complained that for some time now he had not been paid and he had had to rely on one or two of the more proficient students to take one class whilst he took the other. This situation had endured for some time following the departure of his only colleague. This madrassa had not yet been adopted and hence received no resources of any kind from the Regional Directorate surviving therefore on private donations as and when the feeder villages and/or parents were able to make contributions of one thing or another.

It was difficult not to feel that one was witnessing the destruction of the life-chances of these children right before one's own eyes and to be impotent to do anything about it.

Most of the Madrassas visited subsequently were adopted with facilities better than this but often not much better. More often than not staff were unable to communicate directly with me because they were not proficient in English [and this was true too of some of the subject teachers of 'English'] but rather only in Arabic and their tribal languages in which I was sadly not remotely proficient.

Trying Conditions Continue – Frogs:

> 25.10.11: my first job this morning was to let out a frog which had somehow gained entrance to my small house the night before without being spotted by me as I locked up for the night. As I opened my inner fly-screen to let it out I also discovered a toad located between it and the bolted iron and glass outer door. However as I had no power at all last night perhaps this is not so surprising because I had to conduct my lock-up routine for the night by the meagre light provided by my head-torch. Today we have had no power at all except for two short bursts of a few minutes each.
>
> As the wet season continues in the evenings, when entering and leaving my house, I always have to be careful not to tread on the frogs that gather in numbers outside my fly-screen door - their croaking is often incessant. They station themselves there in order to catch the insects that are attracted by the light within - when I have it.

Moore writes:

> ... *In the rainy season, at night, the frogs of which there are vast numbers and much larger than those in England, make as much noise as a pack of hounds ...*

Learning by Rote

A teaching method commonly encountered here is to get children to learn things by rote. With this objective a teacher will often train the whole class to chant a piece of information after he or she has recited it. A class will also be taught that it is polite to welcome a visitor to their classroom, especially those considered to be of some importance. The class will be taught to deliver a particular salutation as a group. These practices can sometimes produce a strange result.

Recently on a visit to a school in the bush I entered a classroom causing the children to spring to their feet chanting in their slow and melodic way:

'Good-mor-ning dear vees-i-tor yor-are weal-come-to our-class-room. We are vee-ry- pleased- tu-see-yor.'

I responded by saying:

'Thank you very much. I am pleased to be here.'

To which the children chanted in response:

'Thank-yor-vee-ry-march. I-am pleased- tu-be-hir.'

Grasping their misunderstanding I said:

'No you don't understand – I am just answering your greeting.'

To which they replied:

'Nor-yor don't-un-der-stand. I-am-just-an-swe-ring your-gree-ting.'

Realising the impasse and having forgotten the original purpose of my visit I decided to retreat gracefully from the situation saying:

'Thank you I must go now. It was lovely to meet you.'

As I walked across the playground and away from the classroom I could hear the children chanting behind me growing a little fainter with each step:

'Thank-yor-I-must-gor-now. Eet- was love-ly tu ...'

To the Coast Once More

Another trip to the coast on NGO business and en route on the Barra ferry today, as we stood in the hard sunlight crowded together amidst the choking diesel fumes issuing from the vessel's deck mounted engine housing, I succumbed finally to the **shoeshine boy's pleas** for me to employ his services to polish and repair my boots. I winced as I watched his hardened fingers push a saddler's needle through my boot soles and up into the leather uppers – I half expected to see the needle pass through his own hand instead of through the tough leather of my boots. When I asked him how much I owed him, a conversation that should have taken place before the work was commenced, he said 'You pay me what you like' – an answer designed to flush out any tourist who had not yet learnt the value of goods and services here. I felt in my pocket and discovered that the smallest note I had was one for fifty dalasi – probably five times what I needed to pay. Instead of asking for change I decided to make his day by offering it all to him – although its value in sterling was little more than a pound. This caused a stir amongst onlookers at least two of whom persuaded him to polish their shoes for free as a kind of penalty for doing so well out of the foolish *toubab*.

Back Up-Country

Thanksgiving: 24.11.11 – I have attended my first Thanksgiving dinner!! **Katie hosted Joanna, Steph and me** at her adobe hut in her Fulah village just across the river close to the ferry point at Lamin Koto. My dining partners were all Peace Corps volunteers. Everyone was able to contribute something including Katie who managed to find some frozen chicken in Janjanbureh and myself who managed to obtain a couple of bottles of wine which turned out to be more drinkable than I anticipated. We were well entertained by my dinner companions' various explanations of the origins of Thanksgiving – the improvised Native American and Settlers' headgear which we all wore helped – it having been constructed by Katie ahead of the event from whatever she could find.

In the course of the meal we heard amongst other things about Katie's experience of being present at a birth in her village – a privilege afforded her by the fact that she had been helping the mother during her pregnancy. There is a tradition here that a woman giving birth must not cry out no matter how painful labour and delivery. We heard that the mother in question on this occasion did not.

Moore says too that:

> ... *it is usual to see the women abroad the same day or the morrow after they are delivered ...*

So there we were, we volunteer cousins from either side of The Pond, like many others in this alien landscape amongst an alien people with grand intent to help, to teach, to support in areas like education, health, horticulture and the rest - relying implicitly on our West African hosts for our personal survival on a daily basis.

I thought of the Thanksgiving story I had just heard, of those early years at the Plymouth Plantation in the 1620s and how we are told its survival depended on the help received from its Native American neighbours. From Katie's back yard I looked across a scene that in some ways mirrored that place at that time; a scene that can't have changed much

Thanksgiving dinner with the US Peace Corps – host Katie (centre) with Steph (left) and Joanna (right)

here since those early days there. In a clearing, across the intervening wattle and daub fencing, over the low adobe buildings, I could see a solitary woman winnowing millet in the time honoured way. She was throwing it up in the air from her flat woven tray and catching it again so that the breeze could carry away the chaff.

I thought of the great blessing of mankind at its best working in spite of difference to help one another.

I don't think chicken, vegetables and wine ever tasted so good!

Departure Confirmed: November 2011: Following recent correspondence/discussion with both the Permanent Secretary at the Ministry of Basic and Secondary Education and my Regional Directorate I have now firmed up my departure intentions and will be leaving this country and my life here next month for what should be the last time. I will arrive back in the UK in time for Christmas but will be returning via Dakar where I will be able to spend a couple of days exploring the Senegalese capital and thence, via Brussels, return to Heathrow. Although in many ways this is none too soon – as my tolerance for the demanding conditions here has been steadily and cumulatively eroded and I have slipped into something of a spiritual malaise – it is with some sadness that I leave my African family and indeed this land and its people. I have explained to my *kunda* folk that soon I must go. Though they seem to have received this declaration with some sincere regret amidst pleas from them for me to stay this has not prevented them from bargaining with one another about who gets what of the equipment and other possessions that I intend to bequeath to them.

Faa Bakari cannot understand why anyone would not wish to stay here for the rest of their days. He has presented me with **another set of African clothes** – this time a costume consisting of milk-chocolate coloured pantaloons with matching smock which has an embroidered border in white at the neck and cuffs in a shiny material so locally popular. I will wear this suit for Friday-best this week and try to find room for it in my luggage so that it returns to the UK with me.

The Royal African Company Brucoe factory was closed sometime around March/April 1735 there being little trade to be done in the area. By then Moore had moved on to various Company locations along the Gambia and eventually to its factory at Joar on the north Bank close to Cower [Kaur] further downstream.

Up-country Farewells – Return to the Coast

On 8 April 1735 Moore embarked on the Company sloop *James*. Job Solomon a freed slave with whom Moore had struck up an association came down to the sloop with him and they parted with tears in Job's eyes. He arrived at Fort St James and following the finalisation of his company affairs he embarked on 13 May on the *Dolphin Snow* and due to adverse winds, passed out of the river and past Cape St Mary after a further two days.

When **my departure** came at last it felt as if I was rolling up my West African life in reverse to the way I had unfurled it approximately 17 months earlier. First there was my last day at work and much hand shaking with colleagues. Those whom for one reason or another I had missed at the office eventually appeared one by one at my compound for a final individual farewell.

There followed the giving away of almost all my equipment and unwanted belongings. It went item by item to this compound 'brother' or that compound 'sister'. I undertook this with equal consideration to that with which it had been acquired when I arrived. There was also a distribution of money as a gesture of thanks for those who had made my stay so welcoming and comfortable. However this distribution caused something of a stir. Apparently sometimes I had made insufficient distinction between the statuses of the recipients. This was most apparent in the gift of an unwanted suitcase to one of the lower status young ladies. She had been particularly helpful during my stay without complaint or request of favour in return. The suitcase I knew would be highly prized and used, as they frequently were, as a stand-in for a wardrobe which most up-country Africans I came across rarely possessed. Ultimately the compound head Faa

Bakari came to me to say if I had any other parting gifts to distribute would I please do so through him as he would then distribute them in accordance with local protocols. I later learnt that in spite of my allocation the recipient of the suitcase, as she told me herself tearfully, had not been allowed to keep it and it had been re-allocated to someone else.

Then there followed my compound leave taking – I could feel almost before I left that my African family were already beginning to lose a sense of me in actuality; they had perhaps a sense of having to reconfigure their lives without this *toubab* who had lived in their midst for approximately 15 months. I had been almost unknown to them before I arrived. Then, except for a few details they had gleaned from my NGO, I lived only in their imaginations. Now I felt that for them I was returning to that world of ideas where the echo of my present being would be constructed from what they thought they remembered of me with not a little added by themselves. I hoped the memories and additions would be positive.

Seats were at a premium on the green bus, my chosen mode of transport back to the coast, and my *kunda*folk had thoughtfully engaged someone they knew at Bansang, the eastern terminus of its route some twenty or so miles back along the South Bank Road, asking them to occupy a seat for me so that I could pay them for their trouble and fill the seat myself for the rest of the journey westwards.

Out of Africa: Back from the Source

When I arrived back on the coast I spent my last two nights at Mama's Hotel and Restaurant. I spent the time saying goodbye to my African colleagues at the in-country HQ close-by on the first and penultimate morning and enjoyed my solitude thereafter, ingesting deeply this last allowance of reflective time at the end of another phase in my life.

Dakar when I got there seemed positively vibrant with elements of modernity and of course very French compared to relatively small scale, low tempo Banjul with its frugal architectural and other legacies of a British colonial past.

On his **return to England** after a two month voyage Francis Moore :

> ... sent letters to acquaint his friends of ... [his] ... return from Africa which our English people most of them think so unhealthy that white people cannot live there by reason of excessive heat. The next return of post ... [he] ... received a kind letter from ... [His] ... Mother expressing joy and satisfaction ... by hearing of the return of her son whom for four or five years past she had never expected to see again ... Moore says he ... returned God thanks Who through so many dangers had brought me back to safety to my friends, relations and native country.

When I awoke on my first day back in London on a fresh winter's morning just a few days before Christmas there seemed a strange absence of the bleating of sheep and the clucking of chickens, of the clatter of pots being washed under the standpipe in the yard, of the swish of a palm fronded broom on the veranda outside my door – and the minaret had been strangely silent.

There was instead the London traffic roar outside my window, the daily feverish stampede towards the centre of the metropolis both above and below ground as if all life depended on it.

I wondered whether I would ever be able to convey to people just what I had experienced back there and how far in some way I had got close to the heart of things. Now I had come out of Africa back to my own people, my own culture, back to my roots – but in Africa I had been close to something much further back than that, close to the very beginnings of our collective human experience, something more fundamental, more elemental, something timelessly universal and I wondered now how that encounter would go forward with me into an unknown future in a world that could never be quite the same as the one I had left when I started out on my journey.

GOD BLESS THE GAMBIA AND ITS PEOPLE – MAY THEY LIVE IN PEACE AND FREEDOM ALWAYS AND MAY THEY BREAK FREE FROM SUCH ABJECT WANT!

Postscript

23 August 2012: The Gambia executes nine prisoners on death row. They include one woman and three sentenced for treason. These are the first executions to be carried out since 1985. The death penalty was abolished by the former president, Dawda Jawara, but reinstated by President Yaya Jammeh shortly after he came to power through a military coup in 1995 but until now it had never been carried out.

3 October 2013: President Jammeh announces that The Gambia is leaving the Commonwealth proclaiming that it is a neo-colonial institution.

15 November 2013: the President cuts ties with Taiwan when they refuse additional bail-outs.

10 December 2014: the EU cuts aid to The Gambia over human rights concerns.

December 2014: President Jammeh cuts ties with the EU.

30 June 2015: VSO pull out of The Gambia after a presence of 54 years.

23 November 2015 Jammeh bows to international pressure and says he is banning female circumcision with immediate effect. The National Assembly passes legislation to this effect the following month.

December 2015: the President announces that from hence forward the country is to be known as 'The Islamic Republic of The Gambia'.

January 2016: an order that all female government employees must cover their heads is issued by the government only to be rescinded 10 days later in the face of some resistance.

Record levels of migration are reported. In 2016 alone over 10,000 of The Gambia's population of only 1.9m are reported to have crossed the Mediterranean, mainly via the Sahara through Egypt and Libya, in the attempt to migrate to Europe.

1 December 2016: voters go to the polls in the scheduled General Election. For once the opposition parties are united as a coalition under the leadership of Adama Barrow, a real estate developer who had formerly spent time studying the subject in the UK and working as a security guard at Argos on the Holloway Road in London.

2 December 2016: following the blocking of all social media over the election period 'His Excellency Sheikh Professor Alhaji Dr Yahya A.J.J. Jammeh Babili Mansa' concedes defeat to Adama Barrow. The army is deployed to many towns and villages. The army also deploys in Banjul the capital and builds sandbag defences.

9 December 2016: Jammeh rejects the election result.

10 December 2016: Jammeh declares he will contest the result through a petition to Gambia's Supreme Court.

2 January 2016: the Gambian Press Union reports that a radio station critical of Jammeh, namely Teranga FM, has been closed down by the Gambian intelligence agency. The following day the same fate befalls three others.

3 January 2017: the Gambian Electoral Commission chief goes into hiding.

19 January 2017: the new President, Adama Barrow, who had left the country for his own safety, is sworn into office at the Gambian embassy in Dakar, Senegal and Gambian troops are ordered by him to return to their barracks: anyone at large and armed he says will be regarded as a rebel. Later that day Senegalese troops with Ghanaian and Nigerian support on behalf of ECOWAS and with UN Security Council authorisation, cross the border into The Gambia. They halt their advance on strategic locations, including Banjul, to allow time for Jammeh to go peacefully.

21 January 2017: after the expiry of further deadlines Jammeh eventually agrees to go and flies out of the country from Banjul airport bound for Guinea.

23 January 2017: reports emerge that the equivalent of $11 million is missing from state coffers and that the country is in financial distress. Luxury cars and other items are reported to have been seen being

loaded onto cargo planes at the time of Jammeh's departure. There are reports that Jammeh is now in Equatorial Guinea.

26 January 2017: President Adama Barrow returns to The Gambia after ECOWAS troops have spent several day securing key buildings, road junctions etc. in Banjul and elsewhere.

Patrick Dunn

London – March 2017

Some background reading & sources

Achebe Chinua 'Things Fall Apart', Heinemann, London 1958

Achebe Chinua 'No Longer At Ease' Heinemann, London 1960

Achebe Chinua 'Arrow of God' Heinemann, London 1964

Bennett Lindsay 'Travellers - The Gambia' ,Thomas Cook Publishing - 2nd edition 2005

Burton Sir Richard 'Wanderings in West Africa from Liverpool to Fernando Po', Tinsley Brothers, London 1863

Gray Major William and **Dochard** Staff Surgeon 'Travels in Western Africa in the Years 1818, 19, 20 and 21', John Murray, London 1825

Gray J.M. 'A History of the Gambia', Cambridge 1940

Greene Graham 'Journey Without Maps', Heinemann, London 1936

Gregg Emma and **Trillo** Richard 'The Rough Guide to the Gambia' - 2nd edition 2006

Hardinge Rex 'Gambia and Beyond', Blackie and Son, London 1934

Kobek Katharina Lane 'The Gambia and Senegal', Lonely Planet - 4th edition 2009

Manka Foday Jibani 'Janjanbureh: A History of an Island Community 1800 to Present', Rotary International Club, Spain 2011

Meredith Martin 'The State of Africa: A History of Fifty Years of Independence', The Free Press 2005

Moore Francis 'Travels into the Inland Parts of Africa', Printed by Edward Cave for the author, London 1738

Naipaul V.S. 'The Masque of Africa', Picador, London 2010

Okri Ben 'The Famished Road' Jonathan Cape, London, 1991

Park Mungo 'Travels in to Interior Districts of Africa', Bulmer, London 1799

Park Mungo 'Travels in the Interior Districts of Africa Performed in the Years 1795, 1796 and 1797 with an Account of a Subsequent Mission to that Country in 1805 etc. ... ', Bulmer 1815

Poole Thomas Eyre 'Life, Scenery and Customs in Sierra Leone and The Gambia', D.D. Richard Bentley, London 1850

Reeve Henry Fenwick 'The Gambia: its History, Ancient, Medieval and Modern', Smith Elder, London 1912

Thomas Hugh 'The Slave Trade', Simon and Schuster, New York 1997

www.ingramcontent.com/pod-product-compliance
Lightning Source LLC
Chambersburg PA
CBHW031629160426
43196CB00006B/334